MW00680686

# God's Little Devotional Book

Presented To:

*Carma Hackey*

From:

*Richland Sunday School*

Date:

*May 7, 2000*

CLASS OF 2000

# God's Little
# Devotional Book
# for the Class of 2000

Honor Books
Tulsa, Oklahoma

*God's Little Devotional Book for the Class of 2000*
ISBN 1-56292-898-8
Copyright © 2000 by Honor Books
P.O. Box 55388
Tulsa, Oklahoma 74155

# God's Little Devotional Book for the Class of 2000

# Introduction

Congratulations! As a member of the Class of 2000, you are being launched into the world at one of the most exciting times in recorded history. Speculation abounds, anticipation builds. There is talk of a sparkling new millennium filled with intergalactic exploration and the advancement of new and astounding technologies. What a time to be alive!

At the same time, our world now seems to be a much more challenging and daunting place to live. How do you make good choices when everything around you is moving and changing at breakneck speed? And how do you cut through the hype and determine what's best for your life?

In *God's Little Devotional Book for the Class of 2000,* we offer you insight and wisdom fit for a new millennium. We hope the timeless truths presented in these pages will help you build your life on a firm foundation and make a name for yourself in a new and exciting world filled with limitless possibilities.

GIVE ME A STOCK CLERK *WITH* A GOAL, AND I WILL GIVE YOU A MAN WHO WILL MAKE HISTORY. GIVE ME A MAN *WITHOUT* A GOAL AND I WILL GIVE YOU A STOCK CLERK.

*Fixing our eyes on Jesus . . . who for the joy set before Him endured the cross . . . and has sat down at the right hand of the throne of God.*
*Hebrews 12:2 NASB*

During the days when the United States was taking shape as a nation, Andrew Bradford had an enviable business contract. His company was given the responsibility of doing all the public printing for the new state of Pennsylvania.

Bradford's company had a reputation for sometimes producing shoddy work, and unfortunately, that was the verdict when Bradford was asked to print an important address the governor was planning to deliver. The document was put together in a careless, unimpressive manner.

Another young printer saw this example of sloppy work as a great opportunity. He prepared an elegant document of the speech, and forwarded it with his compliments to the governor and each member of the assembly. He was soon awarded the contract for all of Pennsylvania's public printing. His name? Benjamin Franklin.

Franklin replaced what was inferior with something that was of quality and excellence. That's the mark of a successful product, no matter what it is—even our own emerging life.

# FIND OUT WHAT YOU LOVE TO DO AND YOU WILL NEVER HAVE TO WORK ANOTHER DAY IN YOUR LIFE.

*"Stand at the crossroads and look; ask for the ancient paths, ask where the good way is, and walk in it, and you will find rest for your souls."*
*Jeremiah 6:16 NIV*

A designer in Dallas, Texas, was once asked by a client to build a large, elaborate model. It was one that called for several building interiors and hundreds of human figures. The model was to be created in a scale of one inch to five feet, which meant that each of the human figures was only a little more than an inch in height. Each one had to be hand-painted, using a brush with a single hair.

As the designer hunched over his table one day, painstakingly painting the figures and then carefully gluing them in place, one of his employees asked him, "Don't you find this tedious?"

The designer replied, "Tedious? My goodness, no! I've loved making and painting models ever since I made my first model airplane at age seven. I just can't believe someone is actually paying me to do this!"

Whether you work with your hands or your mind, loving what you do is the secret to having "fun" while you make money. Indeed, work will cease to be "work."

A kindergarten teacher once said about her class of five-year-olds, "They build and tear down and rebuild more in a day than most construction workers do in weeks, but they never call it work. They call it play!"

11

# AH, BUT A MAN'S REACH *SHOULD* EXCEED HIS GRASP.

*This one thing I do: forgetting
what lies behind and straining forward to
what lies ahead, I press on toward the goal.*
*Philippians 3:13-14 NRSV*

Napoleon saw Italy, but not the Alps. He had an objective and he knew where he was going. The Alps were simply something to be crossed enroute.

Washington saw the Hessians massed at Trenton. He didn't see the Delaware choked with ice. A frozen river was simply a challenge to be overcome on the way to a victory.

A young man intent on bettering his life and earning a college degree will hold a strong image of "graduation day" in his mind. The exams, long nights of study, and jobs that must be done to pay for tuition and room and board, are simply the price that is paid in exchange for a great reward.

A mother about to give birth has her mind and heart wrapped around the baby she will soon hold in her arms. The agony of childbirth is simply something that must be endured to experience the joy of new life.

The majority of people will always see the obstacles that loom in their path. But the truly successful will see the objectives—the goals, the reason, the hope that lies beyond the obstacles.

Those who work through problems reside in the land of success. Those who don't, are lost in oblivion.

# NO PLAN IS WORTH THE PAPER IT IS PRINTED ON UNLESS IT STARTS YOU DOING SOMETHING.

*"Write the vision and make it plain
on tablets, that he may run who reads it."*
*Habakkuk 2:2 NKJV*

Henry Ford was once asked, "How can I become a success?" Ford replied, "If you start something, finish it!"

Ford learned this lesson early in his career. When he began work on his first automobile, he worked many long but exciting hours in a little brick building behind his home. Such enthusiasm overtook him, that he found it hard to take time out to eat or sleep. Before he had completed his first car, however, he became acutely aware that he could build an even better car.

He was so sure of the need for improvements that the thrill and enthusiasm for his first car began to lessen. *Why spend all that time finishing a car that he already knew was inferior?* Still, something inside him forced him to continue, to focus his total energy on the first car and finish what he had started, before he allowed himself to fantasize about a second car.

As it turned out, Ford said he learned even more about how to improve the second car by finishing every detail of his original car. If he had given in to the temptation to quit building the first car, he may never have made any car at all.

Many people strive to be perfectionists, but the *completionists* usually accomplish more in life.

# WHEN YOU GIVE GOD YOUR ALL, YOU PUT YOURSELF IN A POSITION TO RECEIVE HIS ALL.

*Go ye into all the world, and*
*preach the gospel to every creature.*
*Mark 16:15*

The story is told of a small dog that was struck by a car and tossed to the edge of the road. A doctor, who just happened to be driving by, noticed that the dog was still alive, so he stopped his car, picked up the dog, and took him home with him. He discovered the dog had suffered only a few minor cuts and abrasions. Reviving the dog, the doctor cleaned its wounds, then carried it to the garage, where he intended to provide a temporary bed.

However, the dog wriggled free from his arms, jumped to the ground, and scampered off. "What an ungrateful dog," the doctor said to himself. He was glad that the dog had recovered so quickly, but was a little miffed that the dog had shown so little appreciation for his expert, gentle care.

He thought no more about the incident until the next evening, when he heard a scratching at his front door. When he opened the door, he found the little dog he had treated. At its side was another injured dog!

Be encouraged! You may never see the difference you make in someone's life, or the difference that person will make in the lives of others, nevertheless, those with whom you share the Gospel will *never* be the same.

17

# NO HORSE GETS ANYWHERE UNTIL HE IS HARNESSED. NO LIFE EVER GROWS GREAT UNTIL IT IS FOCUSED, DEDICATED, DISCIPLINED.

*In a race, everyone runs but only one person gets first prize. . . . To win the contest you must deny yourselves many things that would keep you from doing your best.*
*1 Corinthians 9:24-25 TLB*

18

Charles Oakley, forward for the New York Knicks and an NBA All-Star, has a reputation for being one of basketball's best rebounders. It's his toughness, however, that has probably contributed the most to his outstanding sports career.

While other professional players seem to have frequent injuries, or are sidelined for other reasons, Oakley has had very few injuries over the course of his thirteen-year career, even though he has absorbed a great deal of physical punishment on the court. He is often pushed and fouled. He puts in miles each game running up and down the court. He frequently dives into the stands for loose balls, to the extent the courtside media teases him about being a working hazard. According to Oakley, his tenacity and energy have an origin: his grandfather, Julius Moss.

Moss was a farmer in Alabama who did most of his field work by hand. "Other people had more equipment than he did," Oakley says. "He didn't have a tractor, but he got the work done. No excuses." Moss, who died in 1990, developed all sorts of aches and pains in his life, but he laughed at them and went about his business. Oakley saw a lesson in that—nothing should prevent him from earning a day's pay.

Being focused, dedicated, and disciplined will make the difference between a mediocre life and a *great* life.

19

# I HAVE NEVER BEEN HURT BY ANYTHING I DIDN'T SAY.

*Don't talk so much. You keep putting your foot in your mouth. Be sensible and turn off the flow!*
*Proverbs 10:19 TLB*

20

A young attorney, just out of law school and beginning his first day on the job, sat down in the comfort of his brand-new office with a great sigh of satisfaction. He had worked long and hard to savor such a moment. Then, noticing a prospective client coming toward his door, he began to look busy and energetic. Opening his legal pad and uncapping his pen, he picked up the telephone, and cradling it under his chin, he began to write furiously as he said, "Look, Harry, about that amalgamation deal. I think I better run down to the factory and handle it personally. Yes. No. I don't think three million dollars will swing it. We better have Smith from Los Angeles meet us there. Okay. Call you back later."

Hanging up the phone, he put down his pen, looked up at his visitor, stood, extended his hand, and said in his most polite but confident attorney's voice, "Good morning. How might I help you?"

The prospective client replied, "Actually, I'm just here to hook up your phone."

Many a foible or flaw

Need not show . . . for

If you don't say so,

Others won't know!

There's an old saying that goes, "A shut mouth gathers no foot." Sometimes the best thing to do is just keep your mouth shut!

21

# WE TOO OFTEN LOVE THINGS AND USE PEOPLE, WHEN WE SHOULD BE USING THINGS AND LOVING PEOPLE.

*Be devoted to one another in brotherly love.*
*Honor one another above yourselves.*
*Romans 12:10 NIV*

One day, a boy at summer camp received a box of cookies from his mother. He ate a few, then placed the box under his bed. The next day, he discovered the cookies were gone. Later, a counselor who had been told of the theft saw a boy sitting behind a tree eating the stolen cookies. He sought out the victim and said, "Bill, I know who stole your cookies. Will you help me teach him a lesson?" The boy replied, "Well, I guess—but aren't you going to punish him?"

The counselor said, "Not directly—that would only make him hate you. I have an idea. But first I want you to ask your mother to send some more cookies." The boy did as the counselor asked, and a few days later, another box of cookies arrived.

The counselor then said, "The boy who stole your cookies is by the lake. I suggest you go down there and share your cookies with him." The boy protested, "But he's the one who stole the first ones from me!" "I know," said the counselor. "Let's see what happens."

An hour later, the counselor saw the boys come up the hill—the thief earnestly trying to get his new friend to accept his compass in payment for the stolen cookies, and the victim just as adamantly refusing, saying a few old cookies didn't matter all that much!

Often the best way to "get back at someone" is to show them God's love. You can usually make a friend in the process.

23

# WHEN YOU FLEE TEMPTATIONS, DON'T LEAVE A FORWARDING ADDRESS.

*Now flee from youthful lusts, and
pursue righteousness . . . with those
who call on the Lord from a pure heart.*
2 Timothy 2:22 NASB

Velazquez Polk and Janet Kuzmaak both grew up in Portland, Oregon, but the two couldn't have been more different. Polk was a tough street kid who joined a gang at age ten and was eventually arrested for selling drugs.

Kuzmaak was an honor roll student from an upper-class neighborhood. In 1980, Kuzmaak's sister was raped and strangled to death. Authorities never found her killer. She came to regard every criminal as her sister's murderer.

Kuzmaak eventually became a nurse at a major medical center. Polk, released from jail in 1990, was given a job as her surgical aide. She was furious. She didn't believe in rehabilitation for criminals. But she noticed that when Polk's gang-member friends tried to entice him to rejoin their ranks, he refused. He told Kuzmaak he wanted to flee his old life and join a program to become a nurse's aide. She remembered that her sister had once befriended a man on parole, so she lobbied the hospital to pay Polk's tuition while she continued to monitor him.

Today, she and Polk are great friends. She helped him gain entrance into a world that he once did not know existed. He helped sweep away the bitterness that had once poisoned her heart.

Change and growth are always possible if you first turn away from evil, determined not to return.

25

# WHATEVER YOU DISLIKE IN ANOTHER PERSON, TAKE CARE TO CORRECT IN YOURSELF.

*Why do you look at the speck of sawdust in your brother's eye and pay no attention to the plank in your own eye?*
*Matthew 7:3 NIV*

In *A Closer Walk,* Catherine Marshall writes: "One morning last week He gave me an assignment: for one day I was to go on a 'fast' from criticism. I was not to criticize anybody about anything."

"For the first half of the day, I simply felt a void, almost as if I had been wiped out as a person. This was especially true at lunch . . . . I listened to the others and kept silent . . . . In our talkative family no one seemed to notice. Bemused, I noticed that my comments were not missed. The federal government, the judicial system, and the institutional church could apparently get along fine without my penetrating observations. But still I didn't see what this fast on criticism was accomplishing—until mid-afternoon."

"That afternoon, a specific, positive vision for this life was dropped into my mind with God's unmistakable hallmark on it—joy! Ideas began to flow in a way I had not experienced in years. Now it was apparent what the Lord wanted me to see. My critical nature had not corrected a single one of the multitudinous things I found fault with. What it had done was to stifle my own creativity."

Before you are tempted to criticize someone, examine your own life. While you may not commit the same act or have the same habit you're about to criticize, you probably have some behavior that *could* be criticized. Don't stifle your creativity with criticism!

# SHOOT FOR THE MOON. EVEN IF YOU MISS IT YOU WILL LAND AMONG THE STARS.

*Aim for perfection.*
*2 Corinthians 13:11 NIV*

28

A young man who was confused about his future and in a quandary as to which direction to take with his life, sat in a park watching squirrels scamper among the trees. Suddenly, a squirrel jumped from one high tree to another. It appeared to be aiming for a limb so far out of reach that the leap looked like suicide. As the young man had anticipated, the squirrel missed its mark, but it landed, safe and unconcerned, on a branch several feet lower. Then it climbed to its goal, and all was well.

An old man sitting on the other end of the bench remarked, "Funny, I've seen hundreds of 'em jump like that, especially when there are dogs all around and they can't come down to the ground. A lot of 'em miss, but I've never seen any hurt in trying." Then he chuckled and added, "I guess they've got to risk it if they don't want to spend their whole life in one tree."

The young man thought, *A squirrel takes a chance. Do I have less nerve than a squirrel?* He made up his mind in that moment to take the risk he had been thinking about. Sure enough, he landed safely, in a position higher than he had even dared to imagine.

What dream are you aiming for? Does it seem out of reach? Take a leap of faith. God will always catch you if you fall.

29

# THE SECRET OF SUCCESS IS TO DO THE COMMON THINGS UNCOMMONLY WELL.

*Seest thou a man diligent in his business?*
*he shall stand before kings;*
*he shall not stand before mean men.*
*Proverbs 22:29*

Helping the deaf to communicate was Alexander Graham Bell's motivation for his life's work, perhaps because his mother and wife were both deaf. "If I can make a deaf-mute talk," Bell said, "I can make metal talk." For five frustrating and impoverished years, he experimented with a variety of materials in an effort to make a metal disk that, vibrating in response to sound, could reproduce those sounds and send them over an electrified wire.

During a visit to Washington, D.C., he called on Joseph Henry, a scientist who was a pioneer in research related to electricity. He presented his ideas to him and asked his advice: Should he let someone else perfect the telephone or should he do it himself? Henry encouraged him to do it himself, to which Bell complained that he lacked the necessary knowledge of electricity. Henry's brief solution was, "Get it."

So Bell studied electricity. A year later when he obtained a patent for the telephone, the officials in the patent office credited him with knowing more about electricity than all the other inventors of his day combined.

Hard work. Study. Hope. Persistence. These are all "common things." They are the keys, however, to doing uncommonly well.

# DEFINITION
# OF STATUS:
# BUYING SOMETHING
# YOU DON'T NEED
# WITH MONEY YOU
# DON'T HAVE TO
# IMPRESS PEOPLE
# YOU DON'T LIKE.

*But they do all their deeds to be noticed by men.*
*Matthew 23:5* NASB

Guy de Maupassant's *The Necklace* is the story of a young woman, Mathilde, who desires desperately to be accepted into high society. One day her husband, an ordinary man, is given an invitation to an elegant ball. Mathilde borrows a necklace from a wealthy friend to wear to the occasion. During the course of the evening, she receives many compliments from the aristocracy present. Unfortunately, later that night, she realizes she has lost the necklace.

In order to restore the lost jewelry, Mathilde's husband borrows thirty-six thousand francs, tapping every resource available to him. A look-alike necklace is created, and Mathilde gives it to her friend, without telling her what had happened.

For ten years, the couple slaves to pay back the borrowed francs, each of them working two jobs. They are forced to sell their home and live in a slum. One day after the debt had finally been paid, Mathilde runs into her well-to-do friend. She confesses that the necklace she returned is not the one she borrowed, and she learns that the necklace loaned to her had been made from fake gemstones! The borrowed necklace had been worth less than five hundred francs.

Trying to "keep up appearances" almost always leads to "falling flat on your face."

33

# I LIKE THE DREAMS OF THE FUTURE BETTER THAN THE HISTORY OF THE PAST.

*Remember ye not the former things,*
*neither consider the things of old.*
*Behold, I will do a new thing.*
*Isaiah 43:18-19*

34

A man once took his three-year-old daughter to an amusement park. It was her first visit to such a place, and she was in awe at the sights and sounds, but mostly she was thrilled at the whirl and whiz of the rides. She begged her dad to let her ride one particular ride, even though it was considered the "scariest" ride for kids her age.

As she whipped around the corners in her kiddy car, she suddenly wrinkled up her face and let loose with a terrified cry. Her father, who was riding in the car with her, struggled to get her attention. With a big smile, he shouted over the roar of the ride, "This is fun!" When the little girl saw that he was not terrified, she began to laugh. The new experience that was initially terrifying had suddenly become enjoyable. In fact, she insisted on riding the same ride three more times!

What a comfort it is to know that our heavenly Father will not only ride the new rides in life with us, but that the future is never scary to Him. He has good things planned for us. When we look into the future from our perspective, we may become frightened. But when we look at the future from God's perspective, we are far more likely to shout, "Let's go! Isn't this going to be fun?"

35

# THE WAY TO GET TO THE TOP IS TO GET OFF YOUR BOTTOM.

*How long will you lie down, O sluggard?*
*When will you arise from your sleep?*
*Proverbs 6:9 NASB*

One day, in the fall of 1894, Guglielmo retreated to his room on the third floor of his parent's home. He had just spent his entire summer vacation reading books and filling notebooks with squiggly diagrams. Now the time had come to *work*.

He rose early every morning. He worked all day and long into the night, to the point that his mother became alarmed. He had never been a robust person, but now he was appallingly thin. His face was drawn, and his eyes were often glazed over with fatigue.

Finally, the day came when he announced his instruments were ready. He invited the family to his room, and pushing a button, he succeeded in ringing a bell on the first floor! While his mother was amazed, his father was not. He saw no use in being able to send a signal so short a distance. So Guglielmo labored on. Little by little, he made changes in his invention so he could send a signal from one hill to the next, and then beyond the hill. Eventually, his invention was perfected, partly by inspiration, but mostly by perseverance.

Guglielmo Marconi eventually was hailed as the inventor of wireless telegraphy—the forerunner of the radio. He not only received a Nobel prize in physics for his efforts, but also a seat in the Italian senate and many honorary degrees and titles.

You can accomplish anything you set your heart on by combining your vision with hard work.

# YOU ARE ONLY WHAT YOU ARE WHEN NO ONE IS LOOKING.

*Not with eyeservice, as menpleasers;*
*but as the servants of Christ, doing*
*the will of God from the heart.*
*Ephesians 6:6*

Joe Smith was a loyal carpenter who worked almost two decades for a successful contractor. The contractor called him into his office one day and said, "Joe, I'm putting you in charge of the next house we build. I want you to order all the materials and oversee the job from the ground up."

Joe accepted the assignment with great enthusiasm. He studied the blueprints and checked every measurement and specification. Suddenly, he had a thought. *If I'm really in charge, why couldn't I cut a few corners, use less expensive materials, and put the extra money in my pocket? Who will know? Once the house is painted, it will look great.*

So Joe set about his scheme. He ordered second-grade lumber and inexpensive concrete, put in cheap wiring, and cut every corner he could. When the home was finished, the contractor came to see it.

"What a fine job you've done!" he said. "You've been such a faithful carpenter to me all these years that I've decided to show you my gratitude by giving you a gift—this house."

Build well today. You will have to live with the character and reputation you construct.

SUCCESS IN LIFE IS A MATTER NOT SO MUCH OF TALENT OR OPPORTUNITY AS OF CONCENTRATION AND PERSEVERANCE.

*Let us not get tired of doing what is right, for after a while we will reap a harvest of blessing if we don't get discouraged and give up.*
*Galatians 6:9 TLB*

Charles Schwab, one of the first presidents of Bethlehem Steel Company, once told efficiency expert Ivy Lee, "If you can give us something to pep us up to do the things we ought to do, I'll gladly pay you anything you ask within reason."

"Fine," Lee said, "I can give you something in twenty minutes that will step up your 'doing' by at least 50 percent." He then handed Schwab a piece of paper and said, "Write down the six most important tasks you have to do tomorrow and number them in the order of their importance." Then Lee said, "Now put this paper in your pocket and first thing tomorrow morning look at item one and start working on it until it is finished. Then tackle item two in the same way; then item three and so on. Do this until quitting time. . . . Do this every working day. After you've convinced yourself of the value of this system, have your men try it . . . and then send me a check for what you think it is worth." A few weeks later Schwab sent Lee a check for $25,000, calling his advice the most profitable lesson he had ever learned.

In just five years, Lee's plan was largely responsible for turning Bethlehem Steel Company into the biggest independent steel producer in the world.[1]

What are the six most important tasks you have to do tomorrow?

CLASS OF 2000

41

# ONE IMPORTANT KEY TO SUCCESS IS SELF-CONFIDENCE. AN IMPORTANT KEY TO SELF-CONFIDENCE IS PREPARATION.

*Study to show thyself approved unto God,*
*a workman that needeth not to be ashamed,*
*rightly dividing the word of truth.*
*2 Timothy 2:15*

In the 1984 Olympics, heavyweight boxer Henry Tillman planned out a very careful strategy. He decided he would fight defensively, simply warding off his opponent's blows, until he saw an opening for a strike of his own. Minutes into the fight, it became obvious to Tillman that his opponent had planned the same strategy! After the bell sounded ending the first round, Tillman stepped back, dropped his hands, and mentally shifted gears. He recognized that his initial game plan might not work, but he had come prepared with a second plan. He switched to a take-the-offensive mode of fighting, won the match, and ultimately won a gold medal.

Figure skater Kristi Yamaguchi also had a "plan B" for her Olympic bid. Originally, she had planned to perform her most difficult jump—three revolutions in the air and a graceful single-skate landing known as the triple salchow. A slight stumble in the early portion of her routine led her to make a change. She cut the triple salchow to a double, regained her balance, caught up with her music, and then went on to perform another triple jump—the lutz.[2]

No matter how much we rehearse or plan, things don't always go as we desire. True champions are those who are prepared to adapt if necessary and switch to what works.

# EVERY JOB IS A SELF-PORTRAIT OF THE PERSON WHO DOES IT. AUTOGRAPH YOUR WORK WITH EXCELLENCE.

*Daniel was preferred above the presidents and princes, because an excellent spirit was in him.*
*Daniel 6:3*

Long ago, a band of minstrels lived in a faraway land. They traveled from town to town, singing and playing their music in hopes of making a living. But they had not been doing well financially. Times were hard, and the common people had little money to spend on concerts, even though their fee was small.

The group met one evening to discuss their plight. "I see no reason for opening tonight," one said. "It's snowing, and no one will come out on a night like this." Another said, "I agree. Last night we performed for just a handful. Even fewer will come tonight."

The leader of the troupe responded, "I know you are discouraged. I am too. But we have a responsibility to those who might come. We will go on, and we will do the best job of which we are capable. It is not the fault of those who come that others do not. They should not be punished with less than our best."

Heartened by his words, the minstrels gave their best performance ever. After the show, the old man called his troupe to him again. In his hand was a note, handed to him by one of the audience members just before the doors closed behind him. Slowly the man read, "Thank you for a beautiful performance." It was signed simply, "Your King."

Everything you do is performed before your king— the King of kings. Are all of your words and deeds worthy of His audience?

# THE BEST THINGS IN LIFE ARE NOT FREE.

*Forasmuch as ye know that ye were not redeemed
with corruptible things, as silver and gold. . . .
But with the precious blood of Christ, as of
a lamb without blemish and without spot.*
1 Peter 1:18-19

For years, Arthur Blessit has carried a six-by-ten foot, 80-pound cross on his shoulders through towns and cities around the world. "It blows people's minds," he says. Once he has gained people's attention, he finds he has a unique opportunity to share the Gospel.

Blessit first became well known for preaching to the hippies of Hollywood's Sunset Strip. He gained national attention when he undertook a cross-carrying journey—along with four members of his rock group, the Eternal Rush—to Washington, D.C. The 3,500-mile trip took seven months to complete.

As the group traveled, they held rallies. Blessit urged fellow Christians to meet him at the Washington Monument at the end of his trip—but not with empty hands. "Christians need to come and give something," he preached. He asked that people bring or send two gifts for the nation's needy, gifts given openly with "both hands." Those who went to the capital to meet him found a third opportunity to give. This gift was to be made with an open heart and an open vein—at a bloodmobile parked on the site.

While the Gospel message is free to all who will receive it, the giving of the Gospel costs, and continues to cost, a great deal!

47

# YOU CAN LEAD A BOY TO COLLEGE, BUT YOU CANNOT MAKE HIM THINK.

*It is senseless to pay tuition to educate
a rebel who has no heart for truth.*
Proverbs 17:16 TLB

48

At Princeton, Woodrow Wilson was first a teacher, and later, president of the university. Although he was popular with the students, he did have a reputation for cracking down on students who were not serious in their pursuit of an education.

The mother of one young man who was expelled for cheating made a trip to Princeton to talk with Wilson. She pleaded with him to reinstate her son because of the possible adverse reaction his expulsion would have on her own health and reputation. She told him of an impending operation and said she felt certain she would die if her son were not readmitted. Wilson heard her pleas and then responded, taking a very tough stance, "Madam, you force me to say a hard thing. If I had to choose between your life or my life or anybody's life and the good of this college, I should choose the good of the college."

Failure to study and to apply oneself fully to one's studies is a form of rebellion. The same holds for cheating. Do your best in school. Don't blame a teacher for being too hard on you, when the blame actually lies in your being too easy on yourself. Learn to be a thinker!

# IF A MAN CANNOT BE A CHRISTIAN IN THE PLACE WHERE HE IS, HE CANNOT BE A CHRISTIAN ANYWHERE.

*Don't work hard only when your master is watching and then shirk when he isn't looking; work hard and with gladness all the time, as though working for Christ, doing the will of God with all your hearts.*

*Ephesians 6:6-7 TLB*

50

In an extensive opinion survey, *The Day America Told the Truth,* James Patterson and Peter Kim reported some startling findings:

- Only 13% saw all Ten Commandments as binding and relevant.

- 91% lied regularly, both at work and home.

- Most workers admitted to goofing off an average of seven hours a week.

- About half of the workforce admitted they regularly called in sick even when they felt well.

When they were asked what they would be willing to do for 10 million dollars, 25% said they would abandon their families, 23% would be prostitutes for a week, and 7% would murder a stranger!

Lest you conclude that the people they surveyed were all ungodly criminals, two other statisticians, Doug Sherman and William Hendricks, found that Christians were almost as likely as unbelievers to do such things as steal from the workplace, falsify their income tax, and selectively obey laws.

To truly claim to be a Christian, a person must do far more than go to church occasionally. He or she must strive to be Christlike 24 hours a day, 365 days a year, in all situations and all circumstances.

# DON'T ASK GOD FOR WHAT YOU THINK IS GOOD; ASK HIM FOR WHAT HE THINKS IS GOOD FOR YOU.

*After this manner therefore pray ye. . . .*
*Thy kingdom come. Thy will be done*
*in earth, as it is in heaven.*
*Matthew 6:9-10*

During a prayer meeting one night, an elderly woman pleaded, "It really doesn't matter what You do with us, Lord, just have Your way with our lives." Adelaide Pollard, a rather well-known itinerant Bible teacher, overheard her prayer. At the time, she was deeply discouraged because she had been unable to raise the money she needed to go to Africa for missionary service. She was moved by this woman's sincere request of God, and when she went home that evening, she meditated on Jeremiah 18:3-4:

*Then I went down to the potter's house, and behold, he wrought a work on the wheel, and the vessel that he made of clay was marred in the hand of the potter; so he made it again another vessel, as seemed good to the potter to make it.*

Before retiring, Adelaide took pen in hand and wrote in hymn form her own prayer:

"Have Thine own way, Lord! Have Thine own way! Thou art the potter, I am the clay. Mold me and make me after Thy will, while I am waiting, yielded and still.

"Have Thine own way, Lord! Have Thine own way! Search me, and try me, Master, today! Whiter than snow, Lord, wash me just now, as in Thy presence humbly I bow."

The best way to discover the purpose for your life and how to do it is to give your whole life to God. Then he can fulfill His plan for you.

# OPPORTUNITIES ARE SELDOM LABELED.

*Seek, and ye shall find; knock,*
*and it shall be opened unto you.*
Matthew 7:7

54

In 1970, Wally started baking chocolate chip cookies for his friends using a recipe and procedure that had been passed down from his Aunt Della. For five years, he gave away every batch he made, even though people often told him that his cookies were so good that he should go into business and sell them. Wally had other ideas though. He was determined to become a big-time show business manager.

Then one day a friend, B.J. Gilmore, told him that she had a friend who could put up the money for a cookie-making business. Her friend never made the investment, but Wally got some of his own friends—including Jeff Wall, Helen Reddy, and Marvin Gaye—to put up some money. Then Wally was off and running.

Originally, he intended to open up only one store on Sunset Boulevard, just enough to "make a living." After all, his was the only store in the world dedicated to the sale of nothing but chocolate chip cookies. But business grew virtually overnight. Wally's "Famous Amos Chocolate Chip Cookies" were soon distributed worldwide. Wally himself became a spokesman for other products, from eggs to airlines to a telephone company. While he once dreamed of managing stars, he now is one in his own right!

Sometimes dreams come through the back door. Keep it unlocked!

# THE WISE DOES AT ONCE WHAT THE FOOL DOES AT LAST.

*He that gathereth in summer is a wise son:*
*but he that sleepeth in harvest is*
*a son that causeth shame.*
*Proverbs 10:5*

An old legend recounts how Satan once called three of his top aides to a special meeting so that they might make a plan about how to stop the effectiveness of a particular group of Christians. One of the aides, Resentment, proposed, "We should convince them there is no God." Satan sneered at Resentment and replied, "That would never work. They know there's a God."

Bitterness then spoke up: "We'll convince them that God does not really care about right or wrong." Satan thought about the idea for a few moments but then rejected it. "Too many know that God does care," he finally said.

Malice then proposed his idea. "We'll let them go on thinking there is a God and that He cares about right and wrong. But we will keep whispering that there is no hurry, there is no hurry, there is no hurry."

Satan howled with delight! The plan was adopted, and Malice was promoted to an even higher position in Satan's malevolent hierarchy.

Who can tell how many souls have been lost or lives sorely wounded because someone has held to the commonly acceptable notion: *Delay is okay*.

# NOTHING GREAT WAS EVER ACHIEVED WITHOUT ENTHUSIASM.

*The joy of the LORD is your strength.*
*Nehemiah 8:10*

After years of working in Rome on life-size sculptures, Michelangelo went to Florence, where a large block of splendid white Carrara marble had been obtained for a colossal statue. Within weeks, he had signed an agreement to complete a rendition of David for the cathedral. Contract in hand, he started in at once, working with a furious energy so great that he often slept in his clothes, resenting the time it took to take them off and put them on again. He faultlessly examined and precisely measured the marble to see what pose it could accommodate. He made sketches of possible attitudes and careful, detailed drawings from models. He tested his ideas in wax on a small scale. When he was finally satisfied with his design, only then did he pick up a chisel and mallet.

Michelangelo approached painting the ceiling of the Sistine Chapel with the same intensity. He took only a month to develop the theme, then launched with a fury into the final design, building scaffolding, and hiring helpers. Lying at uncomfortable angles on hard boards, breathing the suffocating air just under the vault—plaster dust inflaming his eyes and irritating his skin—he spent much of the next four years literally sweating in physical distress as he worked.

May you do your work with the same passionate enthusiasm!

# TRUST IN YOURSELF AND YOU ARE DOOMED TO DISAPPOINTMENT; BUT TRUST IN GOD, AND YOU ARE NEVER TO BE CONFOUNDED IN TIME OR ETERNITY.

*It is better to take refuge in the LORD than to trust in man.*
*Psalm 118:8 NIV*

Marian had her sights set on becoming a concert singer, a challenge that was doubly difficult because of the color of her skin. Her mother, however, had a patient trust in God. Marian later said, "Mother's religion made her believe that she would receive what was right for her to have if she was conscientious in her faith. If it did not come, it was because He had not considered it right for her. We grew in this atmosphere of faith that she created. . . . We believed as she did because we wanted the same kind of haven in the time of storm."

When Marian was denied admission to a famous music conservatory on account of her race, her mother calmly said that "someone would be raised up" to help her accomplish what she had hoped to do at the conservatory. That someone arrived only a few weeks later. One of Philadelphia's most outstanding voice teachers, Guiseppe Boghetti, made room for her to become one of his students.

Marian Anderson was on her way to becoming one of the most magnificent singers of the twentieth century. On Easter Sunday in 1939, she sang for more than 75,000 people gathered in front of the Lincoln Memorial and gave a performance never forgotten by those who were there. Trusting her future to God, she accomplished more than she could have dreamed.

Regardless of the opposition you encounter in reaching your dream, always remember that God is on your side.

CLASS OF 2000

# DON'T BE DISCOURAGED; EVERYONE WHO GOT WHERE HE IS, STARTED WHERE HE WAS.

*Though your beginning was insignificant,*
*Yet your end will increase greatly.*
*Job 8:7 NASB*

During the late 1960s, a couple was vacationing in the California mountains one day and they noticed a pleasant-appearing young man sitting by a bridge near their hotel. Day after day they saw him sitting in that same spot. At first, they assumed he was fishing, but after taking a closer look, they realized he was doing nothing—just sitting and staring into space. Finally, on the last day of their vacation, they couldn't stand it anymore. They just had to ask: "Why do you sit in that one spot all day, every day?"

He replied with a smile, "I happen to believe in reincarnation. I believe that I have lived many times before and that I will have many lives following this one. So this life I'm sitting out."

In reality, it's impossible for any of us to "sit out" life. Each day, we are either moving forward or backward, getting stronger or weaker, moving higher or lower. Each of us begins every new day with a fresh opportunity to change tomorrow's "starting point."

You only have one chance at it. What will you do today to make your tomorrow better?

# MATURITY DOESN'T COME WITH AGE; IT COMES WITH ACCEPTANCE OF RESPONSIBILITY.

*When I was a child, I spake as a child,*
*I understood as a child, I thought as a child: but*
*when I became a man, I put away childish things.*
*1 Corinthians 13:11*

A number of definitions of maturity have been offered by experts, but these are perhaps among the best understood by the average person:

Maturity is when you not only want to have a puppy to call your own, but when you remember on your own to give it food and water every day.

Maturity is when you not only know how to dress yourself, but you remember to put your dirty clothes in the laundry hamper after you've taken them off.

Maturity is when you not only are capable of using a telephone to call a friend, but when you know how to keep your calls short so others can have access to the phone.

Maturity is when you not only are old enough to stay at home alone, but when you can be trusted to stay at home and even have friends over.

Maturity is when you are not only old enough to drive the car by yourself, but you pay for the gasoline you use.

Maturity is when you are not only old enough to stay up late, but you are wise enough to go to bed early.

The more you learn to accept responsibility for your life, the more you will grow in maturity. With greater responsibility and maturity comes greater privileges.

# THE MAN WHO WINS MAY HAVE BEEN COUNTED OUT SEVERAL TIMES, BUT HE DIDN'T HEAR THE REFEREE.

*For though a righteous man falls*
*seven times, he rises again.*
*Proverbs 24:16 NIV*

The difference between success and failure is often the ability to get up just one more time than you fall down!

Moses easily could have given up. He had an "interrupted" childhood and lived with a foster family. He also had a strong temper, a stammering tongue, and a criminal record, but when God called to him, he ultimately said yes.

Joshua had seen the Promised Land and then been forced to wander in the wilderness for forty years with cowards who didn't believe, as he did, that they could conquer their enemies and possess the land. He could have given up in discouragement, but he was willing to go when God said to go.

Peter had a hard time making the transition from fisherman to fisher of men. He sank while trying to walk on water, was strongly rebuked by Jesus for trying to tell Him what to do, and denied knowing Jesus in that hour when Jesus needed him most. He easily could have seen himself as a hopeless failure. But when the opportunity came to preach the Gospel before thousands on the Day of Pentecost, he responded.

No matter what you've done, what mistakes you may have made, what errors you may have committed, you're not a failure until you lay down and quit.

67

# THE HAPPIEST PEOPLE DON'T NECESSARILY HAVE THE BEST OF EVERYTHING. THEY JUST MAKE THE BEST OF EVERYTHING.

*For I have learned, in whatsoever state I am, therewith to be content. I can do all things through Christ which strengtheneth me.*
*Philippians 4:11,13*

A story is told of identical twins: one a hope-filled optimist who often said, "Everything is coming up roses!" And the other, a sad and hopeless pessimist who continually expected the worst to happen. The concerned parents of the twins brought them to a psychologist in hopes he might be able to help them balance their personalities.

The psychologist suggested that on the twins' next birthday, the parents put them in separate rooms to open their gifts. "Give the pessimist the best toys you can afford," the psychologist said, "and give the optimist a box of manure." The parents did as he said.

When they peeked in on the pessimistic twin, they heard him complaining, "I don't like the color of this toy. I'll bet this toy will break! I don't like to play this game. I know someone who has a bigger toy than this!"

Tiptoeing across the corridor, the parents peeked in and saw their optimistic son gleefully throwing manure up in the air. He was giggling as he said, "You can't fool me! Where there's this much manure, there's gotta be a pony!"

How are you looking at life today? As an accident waiting to happen, or a blessing about to be received?

# KEEP COMPANY WITH GOOD MEN AND GOOD MEN YOU WILL IMITATE.

*Iron sharpeneth iron; so a man sharpeneth*
*the countenance of his friend.*
*Proverbs 27:17*

A missionary surgeon in one of China's hospitals restored sight to a man who had been nearly blinded by cataracts. A few weeks later, to his great surprise, forty-eight blind men showed up on his hospital's doorstep. They had all come to be cured. Amazingly, these blind men had walked more than two hundred and fifty miles from a remote area of China to get to the hospital. They had traveled by holding on to a rope chain. Their guide and inspiration was the man who had been cured.

The Christian evangelist, Dr. J. Wilbur Chapman, concluded from his study of the New Testament Gospels that Jesus healed some forty people personally and directly. Of this number, thirty-four were brought to Him by friends or family members, or Jesus was taken to the ailing person by others. Only six of the forty people healed in the Gospels found their way to Jesus, or He to them, *without* someone giving assistance.

In the Gospels, Jesus refers to His followers as "friends." To them, He was the Friend of friends, closer even than a brother. Not only do you become like the friends with whom you associate, but when you choose to hang out with friends who are like Jesus, you will find yourself imitating Him more and more.

71

# LEARN BY EXPERIENCE— PREFERABLY OTHER PEOPLE'S.

*All these things happened to them as examples—as object lessons to us—to warn us against doing the same things.*
*1 Corinthians 10:11* TLB

72

Famous World War II general, George S. Patton Jr., was an avid reader and student of history. He wrote to his son in 1944: "To be a successful soldier, you must know history. Read it objectively . . . . In Sicily I decided as a result of my information, observations, and a sixth sense that I have that the enemy did not have another large scale attack in his system. I bet my shirt on that and I was right." His sixth sense may very well have been formed by thousands of hours of reading history and both biographies and autobiographies.

Historical parallels were constantly on Patton's mind. When he observed the situation in Normandy on July 2, 1944, he immediately wrote Eisenhower that the German Schlieffen Plan of 1914 could be applied. A month later, an operation such as he had described brought about the German defeat in Normandy.

The book that perhaps influenced Patton most was Ardant du Picque's *Battle Studies*. Patton used it to help solve the problem of getting infantry to advance through enemy artillery fire. He recommended it to Eisenhower: "First read *Battle Studies* by Du Pique (you can get a copy at Leavenworth) then put your mind to a solution."

Most of the successful men in the world are avid readers, especially of biographies. If you are interested in being a success in life, immerse yourself in the life stories of successful people. You will learn from their mistakes and failures, as well as their successes and triumphs.

# MANY MEN HAVE TOO MUCH WILLPOWER. IT'S WON'T POWER THEY LACK.

*A man without self-control is as defenseless*
*as a city with broken-down walls.*
*Proverbs 25:28 TLB*

In *Sin, Sex and Self-Control,* Norman Vincent Peale writes: "Martha took the kids away to the mountains for a month, so I was a summer bachelor. And about midway through that month I met a girl, a beautiful girl looking for excitement. She made it clear that I had a green light . . . so for one weekend I put my conscience in mothballs and arranged a meeting with her for Saturday night.

"I woke up early Saturday morning with a bit of a hangover; I'd played poker until late the night before. I decided to get up, put on my swimming trunks, and take a walk on the beach to clear my head. I took an ax along, because the wreck of an old barge had come ashore down the beach, and there was a lot of tangled rope that was worth salvaging. . . . There was something about the freshness of the morning and the feel of the ax that made me want to keep on swinging it. So I began to chop in earnest."

As he chopped, a strange thing began to happen. He said, "I felt as if I were outside myself, looking at myself through a kind of fog that was gradually clearing. And suddenly I knew that what I had been planning for that evening was so wrong, so out of key with my standards and my loyalties and the innermost me that it was out of the question." He canceled the date.

Have you exercised your "won't" power lately?

# IT'S NOT HARD TO MAKE DECISIONS WHEN YOU KNOW WHAT YOUR VALUES ARE.

*Daniel purposed in his heart
that he would not defile himself.
Daniel 1:8*

Marshall Field once offered the following twelve reminders to help a person obtain a sound sense of values:

1. The value of time.

2. The success of perseverance.

3. The pleasure of working.

4. The dignity of simplicity.

5. The worth of character.

6. The power of kindness.

7. The influence of example.

8. The obligation of duty.

9. The wisdom of economy.

10. The virtue of patience.

11. The improvement of talent.

12. The joy of originating.

Can you state the core principles of your value system today? For some, it is likely to be the Ten Commandments. For others, it is the sayings of Jesus.

Solid values are like unblemished, evenly-hewn stones. No matter what you build with them, you can be sure that if you follow the basic laws of construction, the structure will be solid and all your decisions will stand firm.

# CONQUER YOURSELF RATHER THAN THE WORLD.

*Similarly, encourage the young
men to be self-controlled.*
Titus 2:6 NIV

When you get what you want in your struggle
for self,
And the world makes you king for a day,
Just go to a mirror and look at yourself,
And see what that man has to say.
For it isn't your father or mother or wife,
Whose judgment upon you must pass;
The fellow whose verdict counts most in your life,
Is the one staring back from the glass.
Some people may think you are a straight-
shooting chum,
And call you a wonderful guy,
But the man in the glass says you're only a bum,
If you can't look him straight in the eye.
He's the fellow to please, never mind all the rest,
For he's with you clear up to the end,
And you have passed your most dangerous,
difficult test,
If the man in the glass is your friend.
You may fool the whole world down your pathway
of years,
And get pats on the back as you pass,
But your final reward will be heartache and tears,
If you've cheated the man in the glass.

—Anonymous

Learn to conquer yourself by developing your self-
control, and you'll be able to look yourself straight in
the eye and know you've done your best.

I AM ONLY ONE; BUT STILL I AM ONE. I CANNOT DO EVERYTHING, BUT STILL I CAN DO SOMETHING; I WILL NOT REFUSE TO DO THE SOMETHING I CAN DO.

*Under his (Christ's) direction the whole body is fitted together perfectly, and each part in its own special way helps the other parts.*

Ephesians 4:16 TLB

Jewish physician Boris Kornfeld was imprisoned in Siberia. There he worked in surgery, helping both the staff and prisoners. He met a Christian whose name is unknown but whose quiet faith and frequent reciting of the Lord's Prayer had an impact on Dr. Kornfeld.

One day while repairing the slashed artery of a guard, Dr. Kornfeld seriously considered suturing the artery in such a way that the guard would slowly die of internal bleeding. The violence he recognized in his own heart appalled him, and he found himself saying, "Forgive us our sins as we forgive those who sin against us." Afterward, he began to refuse to obey various inhumane, immoral, prison-camp rules. He knew his quiet rebellion put his life in danger.

One afternoon, he examined a patient who had undergone an operation to remove cancer. He saw in the man's eyes a depth of spiritual misery that moved him with compassion, and he told him his entire story, including a confession of his secret faith. That very night, Dr. Kornfeld was murdered as he slept. But his testimony was not in vain. The patient who had heard his confession became a Christian as a result. He survived the prison camp and went on to tell the world about life in the gulag. That patient was Aleksandr Solzhenitsyn, who became one of the leading Russian writers of the twentieth century. He revealed to the world the horrors of the prison camps and perils of Russian communism.

One person can truly make a difference. There is something you can do, and only you can do it. God created you with a destiny.

# POLITENESS GOES FAR, YET COSTS NOTHING.

*A kind man benefits himself.*
*Proverbs 11:17 NIV*

In 1865, after General Ulysses S. Grant had moved his occupying army into Shiloh, he ordered a seven o'clock curfew for the city. One distinguished Southern lady, a Mrs. Johnson, was seen walking near the army's downtown headquarters near the curfew time.

General Grant approached her and said, "Mrs. Johnson, it's a little dangerous out there. I am going to ask two of my officers to escort you home."

She replied determinedly, "I won't go."

Grant smiled, went back in to his headquarters, and returned in a few minutes wearing an overcoat that covered his insignia and rank, and therefore the fact that he was a Northerner.

"May I walk with you, Mrs. Johnson?" he asked.

"Why, yes," Mrs. Johnson replied, nearly blushing. "I'm always glad to have a gentleman as an escort."

Mrs. Johnson would walk with a man she saw as a *gentleman,* even though she would not walk with a Union solider. Good manners and genuine politeness go a long way toward "covering" many of our faults, mistakes, and differences.

# WE SHOULD BEHAVE TO OUR FRIENDS AS WE WOULD WISH OUR FRIENDS TO BEHAVE TO US.

*As ye would that men should do
to you, do ye also to them likewise.*
*Luke 6:31*

President Harry Truman had a reputation for having never been sly or disloyal in his life. He stood by a friend even when he risked public ridicule for it.

One of Truman's friends from his army days was Jim Pendergast, whose uncle Tom was the head of the Democratic Party in Kansas City. Jim and his dad urged Truman to run for office—a judgeship in rural Jackson County. A year later Truman did so, and with Pendergast's support, he won the election. As judge, he didn't always agree with Pendergast's practices. Tom once said to a group of contractors who had asked him to influence Truman, "I told you he was the hardheadedest, orneriest man in the world; there isn't anything I can do."

Unfortunately, Pendergast's penchant for horse races caused him to be investigated for income tax evasion. He confessed, was fined, and was sentenced to serve fifteen months in a federal penitentiary. When Pendergast died during Truman's vice-presidency, Truman didn't hesitate to fly to Kansas City for the funeral. "He was always my friend," Truman said of him, "and I have always been his."

True friendship is not based on what a friend does for you, but on what he means to you.

85

# WHO CEASES TO BE A FRIEND, NEVER WAS ONE.

*This people honors Me with their lips,*
*but their heart is far away from Me.*
*Mark 7:6 NASB*

In *Lessons from Mom,* Joan Aho Ryan writes about loyalty in friendship. She says, "We went to one of the local shopping malls recently where Mom ran into two women who live in her development. . . . They greeted her effusively. It was a brief exchange, during which she introduced me, and they were on their way. 'What phony baloney,' she said when they were well ahead of us. Since her remark came from nowhere, I asked her what she meant.

"With obvious disdain, she explained that she has sat under the canopy at her pool on several occasions with these two women and one of their friends, Sylvia. One day, she said, she sat nearby and heard the three of them talking about the wedding reception of Sylvia's daughter the week before. They raved about the food, the flowers, the elegant country club location, the beautiful bride. . . . Mom said Sylvia was obviously beaming with pride.

"'Well, then Sylvia left, and you should have heard them,' Mom said. . . . 'I couldn't believe friends could be that two-faced. They ripped her apart, talking about how cheap she was, her homely son-in-law, the music they couldn't dance to. It was awful. And they call themselves friends,' she clucked. 'Who needs friends like that?'"

Speaking well of others is not only a good way to acquire friends, but to keep them.

# FAILURE IS THE HALFWAY MARK ON THE ROAD TO SUCCESS.

*For he has delivered me from all my troubles, and*
*my eyes have looked in triumph on my foes.*
*Psalm 54:7 NIV*

Did you fall down the first time you tried to walk? Most likely. Did you feel as if you were drowning the first time you ventured into deep water? Probably. Did you hit the ball the first time you swung a bat? Probably not.

R. H. Macy failed seven times before his store in New York became popular.

English novelist John Creasey received 753 rejection slips prior to publishing 564 books.

Babe Ruth struck out 1,330 times, although he is best known for hitting 714 home runs.[3]

Michael Jordon didn't make the cut for his high school basketball team when he was a sophomore. He cried over his failure, but then tried harder. The next year he made the team, and never looked back.[4]

One salesman noted that he made one sale for about every ten "cold calls" he made. Each sale averaged about $1,000. Rather than be discouraged, then, when he was turned down, he'd simply say, "Well, I just made $100." He saw himself as one-tenth closer to a commission.

Don't expect *never* to fail. Expect occasional failure, learn from it, and move a lesson closer to your goal.

# ADVERSITY CAUSES SOME MEN TO BREAK; OTHERS TO BREAK RECORDS.

*If thou faint in the day of adversity,*
*thy strength is small.*
*Proverbs 24:10*

As a senior in high school, Jim averaged a .427 at bat and led his team in home runs. He also quarterbacked his football team to the state semifinals. Jim later went on to pitch professionally for the New York Yankees.

That's a remarkable achievement for any athlete. But it's an almost unbelievable one for Jim, who was born without a right hand.

A little boy who had only parts of two fingers on one of his hands once came to Jim in the clubhouse after a Yankees game and said, "They call me 'Crab' at camp. Did kids ever tease you?"

"Yeah," Jim replied. "Kids used to tell me that my hand looked like a foot." And then he asked the boy an all-important question, "Is there anything you can't do?" The boy answered, "No."

"Well, I don't think so either," Jim responded.

Today, what others see as a limitation is only a limitation if *you* think it is. God certainly doesn't see you as limited—He sees you as having unlimited potential. When we begin to see ourselves the way God sees us, there are no records that we can't break!

# LEARN TO SAY "NO"; IT WILL BE OF MORE USE TO YOU THAN TO BE ABLE TO READ LATIN.

*Just say a simple yes or no,*
*so that you will not sin.*
*James 5:12 TLB*

The former president of Baylor University, Rufus C. Burleson, once told an audience, "How often I have heard my father paint in glowing words the honesty of his old friend Colonel Ben Sherrod. When he was threatened with bankruptcy and destitution in old age and was staggering under a debt of $850,000, a contemptible lawyer told him, 'Colonel Sherrod, you are hopelessly ruined, but if you will furnish me $5,000 as a witness fee, I can pick a technical flaw in the whole thing and get you out of it.'"

"The grand old Alabamian said, 'Your proposition is insulting. I signed the notes in good faith, and the last dollar shall be paid if charity digs my grave and buys my shroud.' [My father] carried me and my brother Richard once especially to see that incorruptible old man, and his face and words are imprinted upon my heart and brain."

People will remember us for our kept promises and our honesty, especially when we could have profited from not telling the truth. The character of your word is your greatest asset, and honesty is your best virtue.

# A MAN WHO WANTS TO LEAD THE ORCHESTRA MUST TURN HIS BACK ON THE CROWD.

*Come out from among them, and be ye separate, saith the Lord, and touch not the unclean thing; and I will receive you.*
*2 Corinthians 6:17*

In 1643, a young shoemaker's apprentice went to Leicestershire, England, for a business fair. While there, a cousin invited him to share a jug of beer with him and another friend in the pub where they had gone to eat. Being thirsty, he joined them.

After each of the men had drunk a glass apiece, the man's cousin and friend began to drink to the health of first this one and then the other. They agreed that the person who didn't join in with their toasts would have to pay for the jug. This shocked the serious shoemaker's apprentice. He rose from the table, took out a coin, and said simply, "If it be so, I will leave you."

At that, he left the pub and spent much of the night walking up and down the streets of the city, praying and crying to the Lord. The Lord spoke to him these words as recorded in his journal: "Thou seest how young people go together into vanity and old people into the earth. Thou must forsake all—young and old—keep out of all, and be as a stranger unto all." In obedience to this command, the young man left his relations and his home and became a wanderer in England. His name? George Fox, the founder of the Quakers.

If you want to be a leader in life, you will reach a day when you will have to turn your back on people who want to waste their lives. Turn toward those who will lead you, and most of all to the One who will lead you—your Father God.

# MEN ARE ALIKE IN THEIR PROMISES. IT IS ONLY IN THEIR DEEDS THAT THEY DIFFER.

*Many a man claims to have unfailing love,*
*but a faithful man who can find?*
*Proverbs 20:6 NIV*

When Teddy Roosevelt was asked to give a speech to the Naval War College in Newport, Rhode Island, on June 2, 1897, his theme was "Readiness." He insisted the only way to keep peace was to be ready for war, and the only way to be ready for war was to enlarge the navy. It was a rousing, patriotic speech. The following February, the *Maine* was blown up, killing two hundred and sixty four sailors, and Americans across the land cried, "Remember the *Maine!*" In April, President McKinley asked Congress to declare war.

For obvious reasons, Americans were not surprised that Roosevelt backed the war effort. Most Americans *were* surprised, however, when Teddy Roosevelt resigned from his position as assistant secretary of the navy three weeks after the war declaration, so that he'd be ready to fight. His friends told him he was crazy for throwing away his political future. His wife was against it. Yet all who knew Roosevelt well knew, even as they made them, that their protests were in vain. He had to join the effort. He later wrote that he wanted to be able to tell his children why he had fought in the war, not why he hadn't fought in it. As far as he was concerned, a person simply couldn't preach one thing and then do another.

That kind of attitude is what will separate you from the pack and cause you to be a great man or woman in life. When your actions line up with your words, a tremendous reputation will follow.

# DON'T CROSS YOUR BRIDGES UNTIL YOU GET TO THEM. WE SPEND OUR LIVES DEFEATING OURSELVES CROSSING BRIDGES WE NEVER GET TO.

*Don't be anxious about tomorrow. God will take care of your tomorrow too. Live one day at a time.*

*Matthew 6:34* TLB

98

During the four-week siege of Tientsin, during the Boxer Rebellion of June 1900, Herbert Hoover helped erect barricades around the foreign compound and organized all the able-bodied men into a protective force to man them. Mrs. Hoover went to work too, helping set up a hospital, taking her turn nursing the wounded, rationing food, and serving tea every afternoon to those on sentry duty. Like her husband, she remained calm and efficient throughout the crisis, and even seemed to enjoy the excitement.

One afternoon, while sitting at home playing solitaire to relax after her work at the hospital, a shell suddenly burst nearby. She ran to the back door and discovered a big hole in the backyard. A little later, a second shell hit the road in front of the house. Then came a third shell. This one burst through one of the windows of the house and demolished a post by the staircase.

Several reporters covering the siege rushed into the living room to see if she was all right and found her calmly seated at the card table. "I don't seem to be winning this hand," she remarked coolly, "but that was the third shell and therefore the last one for the present anyway. Their pattern is three in a row." Then she suggested brightly, "Let's go and have tea."

If you think about it, you will realize most of the things you worry about never happen. Instead of worrying, relax and use your mental energy for more important things.

# HE THAT HAS LEARNED TO OBEY WILL KNOW HOW TO COMMAND.

*The wise in heart accept commands,*
*but a chattering fool comes to ruin.*
*Proverbs 10:8 NIV*

The story is told of a great military captain who, after a full day of battle, sat by a warming fire with several of his officers and began talking over the events of the day.

He asked them, "Who did the best today on the field of battle?"

One officer told of a man who had fought bravely all day, and then just before dusk had been severely wounded. Another told of a man who had taken a hit for a fellow soldier, sparing his friend's life but possibly losing his own. Yet another told of the man who had led the charge into battle. Still another told of a solider who had risked his life to pull a fellow soldier into a trench.

The captain heard them out and then said, "No, I fear you are all mistaken. The best man in the field today was the soldier who was just lifting up his arm to strike the enemy, but, upon hearing the trumpet sound the retreat, checked himself, dropped his arm without striking the blow, and retreated. That perfect and ready obedience to the will of his general is the noblest thing that was done today on the battlefield."

That's the kind of obedience God desires from us—immediate and complete.

# YOU MUST HAVE LONG-RANGE GOALS TO KEEP YOU FROM BEING FRUSTRATED BY SHORT-RANGE FAILURES.

*Let us fix our eyes on Jesus, the author and perfecter of our faith, who for the joy set before him endured the cross, scorning its shame, and sat down at the right hand of the throne of God.*
*Hebrews 12:2 NIV*

In 1877, George Eastman dreamed that the wonderful world of photography might be accessible to the average person. At the time, photographers working outdoors had to carry multiple pieces of bulky equipment and a corrosive agent called silver nitrate. Eastman theorized that if he could eliminate most of this equipment, he would have something.

Working in a bank by day, he spent his nights reading books on chemistry and magazines about photography. He took foreign language lessons so he could read information published in France and Germany. Then with a partner, he began his own company in 1881. Almost immediately, a problem arose with the new "dry plates" he had invented. Eastman refunded the money to those who had purchased them and returned to his lab. Three months and four hundred seventy two experiments later, he came up with the durable emulsion for which he had searched!

Eastman spent many nights sleeping in a hammock at his factory after long days designing equipment. To replace the glass used for photographic plates, he created a roll of thin, flexible material now known as film. To replace heavy tripods, he developed a pocket camera. By 1895, photography was at last available for the "common man."

George Eastman's long-term vision kept him motivated even when four hundred seventy one experiments failed. Keeping your ultimate dream in mind, set short, attainable goals, and before you even know it, your vision will be a reality!

# CLEAR YOUR MIND OF CAN'T.

*I can do all things through*
*Christ which strengtheneth me.*
*Philippians 4:13*

Harry Houdini, who won fame as an escape artist early in the twentieth century, issued a challenge wherever he went. He claimed he could be locked in any jail cell in the country and set himself free within minutes. He had done it over and over in every city he visited.

One time, however, something seemed to go wrong. Houdini entered a jail cell in his street clothes. The heavy metal doors clanged shut behind him, and he took from his belt a concealed piece of strong, but flexible metal. He set to work on the lock to his cell, but something seemed different about this particular lock. He worked for thirty minutes, but nothing happened. An hour passed. This was long after the time that Houdini normally freed himself, and he began to sweat and pant in exasperation. Still, he could not pick the lock.

Finally, after laboring for two hours, frustrated and feeling a sense of failure closing in around him, Houdini leaned against the door he could not unlock. To his amazement, it swung open! *It had never been locked!*

How many times are challenges impossible—or doors locked—only because we think they are? When we focus our minds and energy toward them and strike the word "can't" from our vocabulary, those impossible tasks turn into attainable goals.

105

# THE FUTURE BELONGS TO THOSE WHO BELIEVE IN THE BEAUTY OF THEIR DREAMS.

*Anything is possible if you have faith.*
*Mark 9:23 TLB*

Grace Hopper was born with a desire to discover how things worked. At age seven, her curiosity led her to dismantle every clock in her childhood home! When she grew up, she eventually completed a doctorate in mathematics at Yale University. During World War II, Grace joined the navy and was assigned to the navy's computation project at Harvard University. There she met "Harvard Mark I," the first fully-functional, digital computing machine. Once again, Grace set about to learn how something worked.

Unlike the clocks in her childhood home, however, "Harvard Mark I" had seven hundred fifty thousand parts and five hundred miles of wire! While most experts believed computers were too complicated and expensive for anyone but highly trained scientists to use, Grace had her own idea. Her goal was to make them easier to operate so more people could use them. Her work gave rise to the programming language cobol.

As late as 1963, each large computer had its own unique master language. Grace became an advocate for a universally-accepted language. She had the audacity to envision a day when computers would one day be small enough to sit on a desk, more powerful than Harvard Mark I; and useful in offices, schools, and at home. At the age of seventy-nine, she retired from the navy with a rank of rear admiral. But more important to her, she had lived to see her dream of personal computers come true!

Believe in your dreams. With God, all things are possible.

107

# THE FUTURE BELONGS TO THOSE WHO SEE POSSIBILITIES BEFORE THEY BECOME OBVIOUS.

*The vision is yet for an appointed time . . .*
*it will surely come, it will not tarry.*
*Habakkuk 2:3*

Eniac was one of the first computers to use electronic circuits, which made for lightning-fast calculations. At first, Thomas J. Watson Jr., the former chairman of IBM, saw no use for it. He said, "I reacted to Eniac the way some people probably reacted to the Wright brothers' airplane. It didn't move me at all . . . . I couldn't see this gigantic, costly, unreliable device as a piece of business equipment."

A few weeks later, he and his father wandered into a research office at IBM and saw an engineer with a high-speed punch-card machine hooked up to a black box. When asked what he was doing, he said, "Multiplying with radio tubes." The machine was tabulating a payroll at one-tenth the time it took the standard punch-card machine to do so. Watson recalls, "That impressed me as though somebody had hit me on the head with a hammer." He said, "Dad, we should put this thing on the market! Even if we only sell eight or ten, we'll be able to advertise the fact that we have the world's first commercial electronic calculator."

That's how IBM got into electronics. Within a year, they had electronic circuits that both multiplied and divided, and at that point, electronic calculators became truly useful. Thousands of IBM 604 were sold.

What wasn't yet obvious to Thomas Watson was obvious to the engineer working in the research department. Always keep your eyes and ears open; you never know what you might discover. Look for the possibilities around you.

WHEN I WAS A YOUNG
MAN I OBSERVED
THAT NINE OUT OF
TEN THINGS I DID
WERE FAILURES.
I DIDN'T WANT TO
BE A FAILURE, SO
I DID TEN TIMES
MORE WORK.

*He becometh poor that dealeth with a slack hand:
but the hand of the diligent maketh rich.*
Proverbs 10:4

110

Early in the 1989 basketball season, Michigan faced Wisconsin. With just seconds left in the fourth quarter, Michigan's Rumeal Robinson found himself at the foul line. His team was trailing by one point, and he knew that if he could sink both shots, Michigan would win. Sadly, Rumeal missed both shots. Wisconsin upset the favored Michigan, and Rumeal went to the locker room feeling devastated and embarrassed.

His dejection, however, spurred him into action and ignited his determination. He decided that at the end of each practice for the rest of the season, he was going to shoot one hundred extra foul shots. Shoot 'em he did!

The moment came when Rumeal stepped to the foul line in yet another game, again with the opportunity to make two shots. This time, there were only three seconds left in overtime, and the game was the ncaa finals! *Swish* went the first shot! And *swish* went the second. Those two points gave Michigan the victory and the Collegiate National Championship for the season.

Have you just failed at something? Don't give up. Instead, work harder. Success is possible!

# LUCK IS A MATTER OF PREPARATION MEETING OPPORTUNITY.

*Make the most of every opportunity.*
*Colossians 4:5 NIV*

CLASS OF 2000

We can learn a great deal from the Alaskan Bull Moose. Each fall, during the breeding season, the males of the species battle for dominance. They literally go head-to-head, antlers crunching together as they collide. When antlers are broken, defeat is ensured since a moose's antlers are its only weapon.

Generally speaking, the heftiest moose with the largest and strongest antlers wins. Therefore, the battle is nearly always predetermined the summer before. It is then that the moose eat nearly 'round the clock. The one that consumes the best diet for growing antlers and gaining weight will be the victor. Those who eat inadequately will have weaker antlers and less bulk. The fight itself involves far more brawn than brain, and more reliance on bulk than on skill.

What is the lesson for us? Spiritual battles are inevitable. We each experience "seasons of attack" in our lives. Whether we are the victors or the victims depends not on our skills or brainpower, but on our spiritual strength. What we do in advance of the war determines the outcome of the battle. Now is the time to develop enduring faith, strength, and wisdom. Now is the time for prayer, reading, and memorizing God's Word. Then, when the opportunity comes, you'll be prepared.

113

# JUMPING TO CONCLUSIONS IS NOT HALF AS GOOD AN EXERCISE AS DIGGING FOR FACTS.

*Study to shew thyself approved unto God,*
*a workman that needeth not to be ashamed,*
*rightly dividing the word of truth.*
*2 Timothy 2:15*

Ted Turner is one of the conspicuous personalities of the twentieth century. He turned Channel 17 in Atlanta into the first "Super Station," transmitting its signal to cable systems nationwide via satellite. Soon after, he purchased the Atlanta Braves baseball team and the Atlanta Hawks basketball team. In 1980, he originated cnn, the world's first live, 'round-the-clock, all-news television network. He organized the Inaugural Goodwill Olympic Games in Moscow, has won numerous awards, and has held national and world sailing titles.

About making choices and decisions, Ted has given this advice, "There is a saying, 'Be sure of your information, then go ahead.' My father was the first one who pointed this out to me. . . . Get all the information you can, along with the advice and counsel of people you think are wise. This is a prerequisite for success in the long haul. You should not make decisions until you have complete knowledge about things. [When] you have to form opinions without as much information as you should have, or without firsthand knowledge . . . don't hold hard and fast opinions. When new information becomes available, you should be able to change your mind."

That is wise advice. Jumped-to conclusions are usually based on speculation—not truth. The person who comes out on top is going to be the one who not only knows all the facts, but most importantly, knows the truth.

# THE MOST VALUABLE OF ALL TALENTS IS THAT OF NEVER USING TWO WORDS WHEN ONE WILL DO.

*In the multitude of words there wanteth not sin: but he that refraineth his lips is wise.*
*Proverbs 10:19*

Albert Einstein is reputed to have had a wholesome disregard for the tyranny of custom. One evening, the president of Swarthmore College hosted a dinner held in Einstein's honor. Although he was not scheduled to speak during the event—only to receive an award—after the award was made, the audience clamored, "Speech, speech!" The president turned the podium over to him. Einstein reluctantly came forward and said only this: "Ladies and gentlemen, I am very sorry but I have nothing to say." And then he sat down.

A few seconds later, he stood back up and said, "In case I do have something to say, I'll come back."

Some six months later, Einstein wired the president of the college with this message: "Now I have something to say."

Another dinner was held, and this time, Einstein made a speech.

If you have nothing to say, it's wise to say nothing. If you do have something to say, it's wise to say it in as few words as possible. As the old saying goes, "If your mind should go blank, don't forget to turn off the sound."

# LAZINESS IS OFTEN MISTAKEN FOR PATIENCE.

*Let us lay aside every weight, and the sin which doth so easily beset us, and let us run with patience the race that is set before us.*

Hebrews 12:1

# God's Little Devotional Book

Henry Ward Beecher, one of the most powerful preachers in American history, gave this illustration in one of his sermons:

"The lobster, when left high and dry among the rocks, has no sense and energy enough to work his way back to the sea, but waits for the sea to come to him. If it does not come, he remains where he is, and dies, although the slightest exertion would enable him to reach the waves, which are perhaps tossing and tumbling within a yard of him.

"There is a tide in human affairs that casts men into 'tight places,' and leaves them there, like stranded lobsters. If they choose to lie where the breakers have flung them, expecting some grand billow to take them on its big shoulders and carry them to smooth water, the chances are that their hopes will never be realized."

Laziness is doing nothing, hoping nothing, being nothing. Patience on the other hand, doesn't mean not doing anything. It means working on in hope that what you're waiting for will eventually come to pass, but you will continue to work on even if it doesn't.

ONE-HALF THE TROUBLE OF THIS LIFE CAN BE TRACED TO SAYING "YES" TOO QUICK, AND NOT SAYING "NO" SOON ENOUGH.

*Seest thou a man that is hasty in his words?*
*there is more hope of a fool than of him.*
*Proverbs 29:20*

A man who had been quite successful in the manufacturing business decided to retire. He called in his son to tell him of his decision, saying, "Son, it's all yours as of the first of next month." The son, while eager to take over the firm and exert his own brand of leadership, also realized what a big responsibility he was facing. "I'd be grateful for any words of advice you have to give me," he said to his father.

The father advised, "Well, I've made a success of this business because of two principles: reliability and wisdom. First, take reliability. If you promise goods by the tenth of the month, no matter what happens, you must deliver by the tenth. Your customers won't understand any delay. They'll see a delay as failure. So even if it costs you overtime, double time, or golden time, you must deliver on your promise."

The son mulled this over for a few moments and then asked, "And wisdom?" The father shot back: "Wisdom is never making such a stupid promise in the first place."

Carefully weigh your ability to back up your words with evidence, and be sure you can deliver on a promise before you make it. A large part of your reputation is your ability to keep your word.

# I WOULD RATHER FAIL IN THE CAUSE THAT SOMEDAY WILL TRIUMPH THAN TRIUMPH IN A CAUSE THAT SOMEDAY WILL FAIL.

*Now thanks be unto God, which
always causeth us to triumph in Christ.
2 Corinthians 2:14*

When Honorious was emperor of Rome, the great Coliseum was often filled to overflowing with spectators who came from near and far to watch the state-sponsored games. Part of the sport consisted of human beings doing battle with wild beasts or one another—to the death. The assembled multitudes made holiday of such sport and found the greatest delight when a human being died.

One such day, a Syrian monk named Telemachus was part of the vast crowd in the arena. Telemachus was cut to the core by the utter disregard he saw for the value of human life. He leaped from the spectator stands into the arena during a gladiatorial show and cried out, "This thing is not right! This thing must stop!"

Because he had interfered, the authorities commanded that Telemachus be run through with a sword, which was done. He died, but not in vain. His cry kindled a small flame in the nearly burned-out conscience of the people, and within a matter of months, the gladiatorial combats came to an end.

The greater the wrong, the louder we must cry out against it. The finer the cause, the louder we must applaud.

# CARVE YOUR NAME ON HEARTS AND NOT ON MARBLE.

*The only letter I need is you yourselves! . . .*
*They can see that you are a letter from*
*Christ, written by us . . . not one carved*
*on stone, but in human hearts.*
*2 Corinthians 3:2-3* TLB

124

When Salvation Army officer Shaw saw the three men before him, tears sprang to his eyes. Shaw was a medical missionary who had just arrived in India. He had been assigned to a leper colony the Salvation Army was taking over. The three men before him had manacles and fetters binding their hands and feet. Their bonds were painfully cutting into their diseased flesh. Captain Shaw turned to the guard and said, "Please unfasten the chains."

"It isn't safe," the guard protested. "These men are dangerous criminals as well as lepers!"

"I'll be responsible," Captain Shaw said. "They are suffering enough." He then reached out, took the keys, knelt, tenderly removed the shackles from the men, and treated their bleeding ankles and wrists.

About two weeks later, Shaw had to make an overnight trip. He dreaded leaving his wife and child alone. The words of the guard came back to him, and he was concerned about the safety of his family. When Shaw's wife went to the front door the morning she was alone, she was startled to see the three criminals lying on her steps. One of them explained, "We know the doctor go. We stay here all night so no harm come to you."

Even dangerous men are capable of responding to an act of love! Touched lives are the most important monuments you can leave. When you treat people with that kind of love, you are impressing your name upon their hearts.

125

# A KNOWLEDGE OF THE BIBLE WITHOUT A COLLEGE COURSE IS MORE VALUABLE THAN A COLLEGE COURSE WITHOUT THE BIBLE.

*All scripture is given by inspiration of God, and is profitable for doctrine, for reproof, for correction, for instruction in righteousness: That the man of God may be perfect, thoroughly furnished unto all good works.*
*2 Timothy 3:16-17*

A Bible—carefully read and well-worn—was the most important book in Gerrit's house. His home was a house of prayer, where many tears were shed in intercession for revival in his church in Heemstede. Almost a generation later, his prayers were answered as that very church became the center of an upsurge of faith in Holland—part of the Great Awakening in Europe.

When she was about eighteen years old, Gerrit's great-granddaughter had a dream about him. He was walking through a beautiful park with her, and he said, "When you sow some seed and put it in the ground, this seed will make a plant, and this plant will give seed again . . . You, my dear Corrie, are the daughter of my grandson. . . . You are a plant, blooming from my seed. I will show you something that will never be changed. It is the Word of God." In the dream, he opened his Bible and said, "This book will be the same forever." He then told her, "Plant the seeds from God's Book, and they will grow from generation to generation."

Corrie ten Boom did just that. She planted God's Word in hearts and minds around the world. Information learned in textbooks is continually updated, and courses of study change. But the truths of the Bible are absolutes. Its promises are sure. Plant its seeds in your heart.

# LITTLE MINDS ARE TAMED AND SUBDUED BY MISFORTUNE; BUT GREAT MINDS RISE ABOVE THEM.

*A just man falleth seven times,*
*and riseth up again.*
Proverbs 24:16

When Aaron was eight months old, he stopped gaining weight. A few months later, his hair began to fall out. At first, doctors told Aaron's parents that he would be short as an adult, but otherwise normal. Later, a pediatrician diagnosed the problem as progeria, or "rapid aging." Just as the pediatrician predicted, Aaron never grew beyond three feet in height, had no hair on his head or body, looked like an old man while still a child, and died of old age in his early teens. His father, a rabbi, felt a deep, aching sense of unfairness.

About a year and a half after Aaron's death, the father came to realize that none of us is ever promised a life free of pain or disappointment. Rather, the most any of us has been promised is that we need not be alone in our pain and that we can draw upon a source outside ourselves for strength and courage. He came to the conclusion that God does not cause our misfortunes, but rather, helps us by inspiring others to help.

Out of Harold Kushner's experience came a book that has helped millions, *When Bad Things Happen to Good People*. He says, "I think of Aaron and all that his life taught me, and I realize how much I have lost and how much I have gained. Yesterday seems less painful, and I am not afraid of tomorrow."

When you stop looking at the difficulties in your life as obstacles and start seeing them as stepping stones, you will begin to rise above your difficulties and gain something from them. They will make you stronger and wiser.

129

# THERE IS NO POVERTY THAT CAN OVERTAKE DILIGENCE.

*He becometh poor that dealeth with a slack hand:*
*but the hand of the diligent maketh rich.*
*Proverbs 10:4*

130

A young reporter once interviewed a successful businessman. The reporter asked the man to give him a detailed history of his company. As the man talked at length, the reporter began to be amazed at the enormity of the many problems the man had overcome. He finally asked him, "But how did you overcome so many problems of such great magnitude?"

The old gentleman leaned back in his chair and said, "There's really no trick to it." Then he added, "You know . . . there are some troubles that seem so high you can't climb over them." The reporter nodded in agreement, thinking of several he was currently facing. "And," the wise businessman went on, "there are some troubles so wide you can't walk around them." Again, the reporter nodded. The man went on, raising his voice dramatically, "And there are some problems so deep you can't dig under them." Eager for a solution, the reporter said, "Yes? Yes?"

"It's then," the man concluded, "that you know the only way to beat the problem is to duck your head and wade right through it."

A problem rarely decreases in size while a person stands and stares at it. But when you diligently pursue a solution, your problem is guaranteed to shrink.

# NEVER DESPAIR; BUT IF YOU DO, WORK ON IN DESPAIR.

*As for you, be strong and do not give up,*
*for your work will be rewarded.*
*2 Chronicles 15:7 NIV*

American sports fans watched in awe on Sunday, March 4, 1979, as Phil took to the giant-slalom slopes at Whiteface Mountain, New York. He exploded onto the course and then settled into a powerful carving of the mountainside. Nonetheless, at gate thirty-five, tragedy struck. Phil hooked his inside ski on a pole, went flying head over heels, and crashed in a crumpled heap. The ski team physician described the injury as "the ultimate broken ankle"—a break of both the ankle and lower leg. He had to put the bones back together with a three-inch metal plate and seven screws.

The question was not whether Phil would ever ski again, but if he would ever walk again. Looking back, Phil describes the months after his injury as a time of deep despair. Still, he never entertained doubts about walking or skiing.

After two months on crutches and a high-disciplined exercise program, he forced himself to walk without limping. In August, he began skiing gentle slopes. Less than six months after the accident, he entered a race in Australia and finished second. In February of 1980, less than a year after his agonizing injury, Phil Mahre took on the same mountain where he had fallen and won an Olympic silver medal.

When defeat and despair threaten to overtake you and squash your dreams, keep on going. Eventually, you will overtake defeat with victory and despair with joy!

133

# YOU CAN ACCOMPLISH MORE IN ONE HOUR WITH GOD THAN ONE LIFETIME WITHOUT HIM.

*With God all things are possible.*
*Matthew 19:26*

The Lord appeared to a man named Ananias in a vision and asked him to undertake what Ananias must surely have perceived as a dangerous mission. He directed him to go to the house of a man named Judas, lay his hands on a man named Saul of Tarsus, and pray that he might receive his sight. Saul had been blinded while traveling to Damascus to persecute the Christians there, having the full intent of taking them captive to Jerusalem for trial, torture, and death. Even so, Ananias did as the Lord asked him, and within the hour, Saul's sight was restored.

According to Christian legend, Ananias was a simple cobbler who had no idea what happened to Saul after that day, or how he had changed the course of human history by obeying God in a simple act that was part of Saul's transformation into the Apostle Paul. As he lay on his deathbed, Ananias looked up toward heaven and whispered, "I haven't done much, Lord: a few shoes sewn, a few sandals stitched. But what more could be expected of a poor cobbler?"

The Lord spoke in Ananias' heart, "Don't worry, Ananias, about how much you have accomplished— or how little. You were there in the hour I needed you, and that is all that matters."

Being in the right place at the right time, even if it's only for one hour, can give you the opportunity to change history. In order to be there, you must simply listen and obey.

# IF YOU DON'T STAND FOR SOMETHING, YOU'LL FALL FOR ANYTHING!

*If you do not stand firm in your faith,*
*you will not stand at all.*
*Isaiah 7:9 NIV*

Former President Harry S Truman once remarked that no president of our nation has ever escaped abuse and even libel from the press. He noted that is was far more common than rare to find a president publicly called a traitor. Truman further concluded that the president who had not fought with Congress or the Supreme Court hadn't done his job.

What is true for an American president is also true for everyone else. No matter how small a person's job may be—no matter how low he may be on a particular organizational chart or strata of society—there will be those who oppose him, ridicule him, and perhaps even challenge him to a fight. That is why no person can expect to conduct himself as if he were trying to win a popularity contest. Rather, a person needs to chart the course he feels compelled to walk in life, and then to do so with head held high and his convictions intact. It's simply a matter of taking life in stride to recognize that every person will eventually face the test of ridicule and criticism as he upholds his principles or defends his morals.

It's inevitable that you will be criticized or attacked sometime in your life. But collapsing from *fear* of an attack isn't inevitable. Stand firm in your faith, and the Lord will stand with you!

# THE DIFFERENCE BETWEEN ORDINARY AND EXTRAORDINARY IS THAT LITTLE EXTRA.

*Whatsoever thy hand findeth to do,*
*do it with thy might.*
*Ecclesiastes 9:10*

Country-music star Randy Travis and his manager, Lib, remember the lean days of his career—all 3,650 of them. For ten years, Lib did whatever it took to keep her club open long enough for somebody to discover Travis' talent. For his part, Randy sang his heart out, and when he wasn't singing, he fried catfish or washed dishes in the kitchen. Then it happened. Everything seemed to click for him. He had a hit called "On the Other Hand," an album contract, a tour offer, and a movie deal. He was hot! Everyone seemed to be calling him an overnight success.

Travis notes, "We were turned down more than once by every label in Nashville. But I'm kind of one to believe that if you work at something long enough and keep believing, sooner or later it will happen."

In many instances in life, it's extra effort that makes the difference. Money can buy a house, but loving touches turn it into a home. A sack lunch can be a gourmet meal with a love note tucked inside. A meal is just food, but with candles and flowers, it's an occasion. Do more than is required of you today. Give the extra that makes life truly extraordinary.

# MAN CANNOT DISCOVER NEW OCEANS UNLESS HE HAS THE COURAGE TO LOSE SIGHT OF THE SHORE.

*Peter got out of the boat, and walked on the water and came toward Jesus.*
*Matthew 14:29 NASB*

Two baseball coaches were commiserating about the difficulty of recruiting quality players for their teams. Said one coach, "If only I could find a man who plays every position perfectly, always gets a hit, never strikes out, and never makes a fielding error." The other coach sighed in agreement and added, "Yeah, if we could just get him to lay down his hot dog and come down out of the stands."

Playing life's game to the fullest requires taking risks. Without risk, life has little emotion, little that can be counted as exhilarating or fulfilling.

- To laugh is to risk appearing the fool.
- To weep is to risk appearing sentimental.
- To reach out for another is to risk involvement.
- To expose feelings is to risk exposing one's true self.
- To place ideas and dreams before a crowd is to risk ridicule.
- To love is to risk not being loved in return.
- To live is to risk dying.
- To hope is to risk despair.
- To try is to risk failure.

Yet the person who risks nothing does nothing, has nothing, and ultimately becomes nothing. Don't be afraid to go for it. Get down out of the stands and play ball!

# FADS COME AND GO; WISDOM AND CHARACTER GO ON FOREVER.

*O my son, be wise and stay in God's paths.*
Proverbs 23:19 TLB

142

Many years ago in South Africa, a man sold his farm so that he might spend his days in search of diamonds. He was consumed with dreams of becoming wealthy. When he had finally exhausted his resources and his health, and was no closer to his fortune than the day he sold his farm; he threw himself into a river and drowned.

One day, the man who had bought his farm spotted an unusual-looking stone in a creek bed. He placed it on his fireplace mantle as a conversation piece. A visitor noticed the stone and examined it closely. He then voiced his suspicion that the stone was actually a diamond. The discreet farmer had the stone analyzed, and sure enough, it was one of the largest and finest diamonds ever found.

Still operating with great secrecy, the farmer searched his stream, gathering similar stones. They were all diamonds. In fact, his farm was covered with diamonds just waiting to be picked up! The farm the diamond-seeker had sold turned out to be one of the richest diamond deposits in the world.

The lessons of wisdom can often be learned in the relationships and experiences we encounter every day. Ask God to reveal to you what you need to know in order to live the life He desires. The resources you need are probably right in front of you.

143

# PERSEVERANCE IS A GREAT ELEMENT OF SUCCESS; IF YOU ONLY KNOCK LONG ENOUGH AND LOUD ENOUGH AT THE GATE, YOU ARE SURE TO WAKE UP SOMEBODY.

*Ask, and it shall be given you; seek, and ye shall find; knock, and it shall be opened unto you.*

*Luke 11:9*

We all know the power of gravity. When we drop a hammer, it hits our toes; it never floats upward. We fall down, not up. But what many of us don't realize is that the gravitational *energy* of the whole earth has been estimated to amount to only a millionth of a horsepower! A toy magnet in the hands of a child probably has thousands of times more energy.

What gravity lacks in energy, however, it makes up in tenacity. Gravity simply refuses to let go.

Not only is gravity tenacious, but it has far-reaching effects. Gravitational pull appears to be virtually limitless, reaching across the universe with nearly unimaginable power. Gravitational pull is what keeps the moon orbiting the earth, the planets revolving around the sun, and the sun—along with a billion other stars—rotating around the center of our galaxy like a cosmic pinwheel.

You may not have a great deal of power or energy today, but as the popular phrase states, you can "hang in there."

Don't stop believing! Don't give up hope! Eventually the door will be opened.

CONSIDER THE
POSTAGE STAMP:
ITS USEFULNESS
CONSISTS IN THE
ABILITY TO STICK
TO ONE THING TILL
IT GETS THERE.

*I have fought a good fight, I have finished
my course, I have kept the faith.*
*2 Timothy 4:7*

In March of 1987, Eamon Coughlan was running in a qualifying heat at the World Indoor Track Championships in Indianapolis. The Irishman was the reigning world record-holder at fifteen hundred meters, and he was favored to win the race handily. Unfortunately, with two-and-a-half laps left to run, he was tripped and fell hard. Even so, he got up and with great effort, he managed to catch the race leaders. With only twenty yards to go, he was in third place, which would have been good enough to qualify for the final race.

Then Couglan looked over his shoulder to the inside. Seeing no one there, he relaxed his effort slightly. What he hadn't noticed, however, was that a runner was charging hard on the outside. This runner passed Couglan just a yard before the finish line, thus eliminating him from the finals.

Coughlan's great comeback effort ended up being worthless for one and only one reason, he momentarily took his eyes off the finish line and focused on the would-be competitors instead.

One of the most important factors in reaching your goals in life is to have single-minded focus. Don't let yourself become distracted by what others do or say. Run your race to win!

# IT NEEDS MORE SKILL THAN I CAN TELL TO PLAY THE SECOND FIDDLE WELL.

*He that is greatest among*
*you shall be your servant.*
*Matthew 23:11*

148

People often think of heart surgeons as being the arrogant prima donnas of the medical world. But those who know Dr. William DeVries, the surgeon who pioneered the artificial heart, couldn't *disagree* more. Co-workers at Humana Hospital Audubon in Louisville, Kentucky, describe DeVries as the kind of doctor who shows up on Sundays just to cheer up discouraged patients. He occasionally changes dressings, traditionally considered a nurse's job, and if a patient wants him to stick around and talk, he always does.

Friends say DeVries is an "old shoe" who fits in wherever he goes. He likes to wear cowboy boots with his surgical scrubs, and he often repairs hearts to the beat of Vivaldi or jazz. "He has always got a smile lurking," says Louisville cardiologist Dr. Robert Goodin, "and he's always looking for a way to let it out."

No matter how high you rise, never forget that you started out at ground zero. Even if you were born to great wealth and privilege, you still were born as a helpless babe. Real success comes not in thinking you have arrived at a place where others should serve you, but in recognizing that in whatever place you are, you have arrived at a position where you can serve others.

# A MAN NEVER DISCLOSES HIS OWN CHARACTER SO CLEARLY AS WHEN HE DESCRIBES ANOTHER'S.

*A good man out of the good treasure of the heart bringeth forth good things: and an evil man out of the evil treasure bringeth forth evil things.*
*Matthew 12:35*

After several months of romance, Napoleon and Josephine decided to marry. The notary who made out the marriage contract was one of Josephine's friends. He secretly advised her against marrying "an obscure little officer who has nothing besides his uniform and sword and has no future." He thought she should find someone of greater worth. With her charms, he advised, she might attract a wealthy man, perhaps an army contractor or a business investor.

Napoleon was in the next room while the notary was giving this advice to his beloved. He could hear every word that was said. Still, he did not disclose he had overheard. Years later, however, he had his revenge.

After his coronation as Emperor, this same notary appeared before him on a matter of business. At the conclusion of their appointment, Napoleon smiled and observed that Madame de Beauharnais—now that she was queen of France—had done very well, after all, to have married that "obscure little officer who possessed nothing besides his uniform and sword and had no future."

The notary was forced to agree that Madame, indeed, had done well. As for himself, he was still a notary!

Be careful before you pass judgment on another. You're revealing something about yourself, and your words may come back to bite you.

# IF YOU SUCCEED IN ALL YOU DO, IT'S A SURE SIGN YOU'RE NOT REACHING HIGH ENOUGH.

*Seek those things which are above.*
*Colossians 3:1 NKJV*

One day during the early 1960s, the University of Florida football team was in a practice session. They were running wind sprints for conditioning. One of the large linemen, Jack Katz, had proven himself to be the fastest lineman on the team.

Katz went to Coach Ray Graves and asked if he might be allowed to run sprints with the faster and smaller backfield players. Permission was granted.

For the next several days, Katz managed to finish last in every race with the backfield runners. Nobody was surprised. The coach went to Katz to ask if he wouldn't rather go back to winning against the other linemen, rather than lose every race against the backs.

Katz responded, "I'm not out here to outrun the linemen. I already know I can do that. I'm here to learn how to run faster; and if you've noticed, I'm losing by a little less every day."

Indeed, a lineman's job is not only to break through and scatter the line on the other team, but also to tackle its backfield players. Katz was preparing himself for his ultimate goal: real-game tackles.[5]

When you master one level, go on to the next. It is the only way to keep growing and developing your skills!

153

EVERY MAN'S WORK, WHETHER IT BE LITERATURE, OR MUSIC, OR PICTURES, OR ARCHITECTURE, OR ANYTHING ELSE, IS ALWAYS A PORTRAIT OF HIMSELF.

*As in water face reflects face,*
*so the heart of man reflects man.*
*Proverbs 27:19 NASB*

154

A young man once made an appointment with a well-published author. The first question the author asked him was, "Why did you want to see me?"

The young man stammered, "Well, I'm a writer, too. I was hoping you could share with me some of your secrets for successful writing."

The author asked a second question, "What have you written?"

"Nothing," the young man replied, "at least nothing that is finished yet."

The author asked a third question, "Well, if you haven't written, then tell me, what are you writing?"

The young man replied, "Well, I'm in school right now, so I'm not writing anything at present."

The author then asked a fourth question, "So why do you call yourself a writer?"

Writers write. Composers compose. Painters paint. Workmen work. What you do to a great extent defines who you are and what you become. What does your work say about you? When your work on the outside coincides with who you are on the inside, you have found your true purpose in life and will find ultimate fulfillment.

155

# WHAT WE DO ON SOME GREAT OCCASION WILL PROBABLY DEPEND ON WHAT WE ALREADY ARE; AND WHAT WE ARE WILL BE THE RESULT OF PRECIOUS YEARS OF SELF-DISCIPLINE.

*I keep under my body,*
*and bring it into subjection.*
*1 Corinthians 9:27*

During a homecoming football game against rival Concordia, Augsburg College found itself losing miserably. But late in the fourth quarter, nose guard David Stevens came off the bench and sparked a fire. He initiated or assisted in two tackles, and when a Concordia player fumbled the ball, David fell on it. As he held the recovered ball high, the crowd roared. It was an unforgettable moment for Augsburg fans!

David Lee Stevens was born to a woman who had taken thalidomide, an anti-nausea drug given to many pregnant women in the early 60s that was quickly proven to cause severe birth defects. David's feet appeared where his legs should have started. Abandoned by his mother, David was adopted by a foster family. Bee and Bill Stevens imposed strict rules of behavior on David, nurtured him, and loved him. They insisted he learn to do things for himself, and they never put him in a wheelchair. At age three, he was fitted with "legs."

In school, David became a student leader, made good grades, organized special events, and befriended new students. In high school, he not only played football, but baseball, basketball, and hockey. He became a champion wrestler. When offered handicap license plates, he refused them stating simply, "Those are for people who need them. I am not 'disabled.'"

David was taught to discipline himself, and so he was able to perform, in spite of his apparent handicap. Whatever obstacle may be in your way, self-discipline can help you either rise above it or plow right through it.

157

# OUR DEEDS DETERMINE US, AS MUCH AS WE DETERMINE OUR DEEDS.

*Even a child is known by his actions,*
*by whether his conduct is pure and right.*
*Proverbs 20:11 NIV*

In the fourth round of a national spelling bee in Washington, eleven-year-old Rosalie Elliot, a champion from South Carolina, was asked to spell the word *avowal*. Her soft Southern accent made it difficult for the judges to determine if she had used an a or an e as the next to last letter of the word. They deliberated for several minutes and also listened to tape-recorded playbacks, but they still couldn't determine which letter had been pronounced. Finally the chief judge, John Lloyd, put the question to the only person who knew the answer. He asked Rosalie, "Was the letter an a or an *e?*"

Rosalie, surrounded by whispering young spellers, knew by now the correct spelling of the word. But without hesitation, she replied that she had misspelled the word and had used an *e.*

As she walked from the stage, the entire audience stood and applauded her honesty and integrity, including dozens of newspaper reporters covering the event. While Rosalie had not won the contest, she had definitely come out a winner that day.

We often think that who we are determines what we do. Equally true, what you do today will determine, in part, who you become tomorrow.

159

# WHAT YOU DO SPEAKS SO LOUD THAT I CANNOT HEAR WHAT YOU SAY.

*Show me your faith without deeds,*
*and I will show you my faith by what I do.*
**James 2:18** *NIV*

160

During the Korean War, a South Korean civilian was arrested by the communists and sentenced to execution. When the young communist leader learned that the prisoner in his charge was the head of an orphanage caring for young children, he decided to spare him. But he ordered that the man's son be executed in his place. The nineteen-year-old boy was shot in the presence of his father.

After the war, the United Nations captured the young communist leader. He was tried for his war crimes and condemned to death. But before the sentence could be carried out, the Christian whose son had been killed pleaded for the life of the killer. He argued that the communist had been young when he ordered the execution and that he really didn't know what he was doing. "Give him to me," the man requested, "and I will train him."

The United Nations forces granted the unusual request, and the father took the murderer of his son into his own home and cared for him. The young communist eventually became a Christian pastor.

For good or for bad, what we do speaks loudly. How vital it is that we do what we say!

# ALL VIRTUE IS SUMMED UP IN DEALING JUSTLY.

*He hath shewed thee, O man, what is good;*
*and what doth the Lord require of thee,*
*but to do justly, and to love mercy,*
*and to walk humbly with thy God?*
*Micah 6:8*

To crack the lily-white system of higher education in Georgia in the 1960s, black leaders decided they needed to find only two "squeaky-clean" students who couldn't be challenged on moral, intellectual, or educational grounds. In a discussion about who might be chosen, Alfred Holmes immediately volunteered his son, Hamilton, the top black male senior in the city. Charlayne Hunter-Gault also stepped forward and expressed an interest in applying to the university. Georgia delayed admitting both boys on grounds it had no room in its dormitories, and the matter eventually ended up in federal court. Judge Bootle ordered the university to admit the two, who were qualified in every respect, and thus, segregation ended at the university level in that state, and soon, the nation.

Attorney General Robert Kennedy declared in a speech not long after: "We know that it is the law which enables men to live together, that creates order out of chaos. . . . And we know that if one man's rights are denied, the rights of all are endangered."

Justice may be universal, but it always begins at the individual level. Is there someone that you might treat more justly today?

# NO MATTER WHAT A MAN'S PAST MAY HAVE BEEN, HIS FUTURE IS SPOTLESS.

*Forgetting those things which are behind, and
reaching forth unto those things which are before.*
*Philippians 3:13*

164

Willingway Hospital is one of the nation's top treatment centers for alcoholism and drug addiction. There would be no Willingway, however, if it weren't for Dot and John, who at one time seemed the least likely candidates to found such a hospital. Early in their courtship, Dot and John drank heavily, and after they married, they began taking amphetamines. John, a medical doctor, was arrested for writing himself narcotics prescriptions. He spent six months in prison, eventually falling on his knees and crying out to God for help in overcoming his addictions.

When John returned to medical practice drug-free and alcohol-free, he began to receive referrals from other doctors to treat their alcoholic patients. Dot and John set up three beds under the chandelier in their own dining room as a detox room. Among their patients have been three of their own four children, each of whom struggled with addictions.

As word of their compassion spread, they established a forty-bed hospital on eleven acres close to their home. The chandelier still hangs in the detox room as a symbol of hope. All four children have worked on the medical staff or administration of Willingway. With God's help, they truly became a family in "full recovery."

Regardless of our past, the future is a blank slate, waiting to be written upon.

# ONE OF LIFE'S GREAT RULES IS THIS: THE MORE YOU GIVE, THE MORE YOU GET.

*The liberal soul shall be made fat: and he that watereth shall be watered also himself.*
Proverbs 11:25

Three young men were each given three kernels of corn by a wise old sage, who admonished them to go out into the world and use the corn to bring themselves good fortune.

The first young man put his three kernels of corn into a bowl of hot broth and ate them. The second thought, *I can do better than that,* and he planted his three kernels of corn. Within a few months, he had three stalks of corn. He took the ears of corn from the stalks, boiled them, and had enough corn for three meals.

The third man said to himself, *I can do better than that!* He also planted his three kernels of corn, but when his three stalks of corn produced, he stripped one of the ears and replanted all of the seeds in it, gave the second ear of corn to a sweet maiden, and ate the third. His one full ear's worth of replanted corn kernels gave him two hundred stalks of corn! And the kernels of these he continued to replant, setting aside only a bare minimum to eat. He eventually planted a hundred acres of corn. With his fortune, he not only won the hand of the sweet maiden but also purchased the land owned by the sweet maiden's father. He never hungered again.

If you want to receive in life, you must first learn to give.

167

# EVERYTHING COMES TO HIM WHO HUSTLES WHILE HE WAITS.

*We do not want you to become lazy,*
*but to imitate those who through faith and*
*patience inherit what has been promised.*
**Hebrews 6:12** *NIV*

In 1928, a happy, ambitious young nursing student was diagnosed with tuberculosis. Her family sent her to a nursing home in Saranac Lake for several months of "curing." She would remain in bed for twenty-one years! Most people may have given up, but not Isabel Smith. She approached the threshold of death on several occasions, but she never ceased to pursue the art of living. She read voraciously, loved to write letters, studied geography, and taught other patients to read and write. From her bed, she studied atomic energy with a fellow patient, a young physicist, and organized a town hall on the topic.

While ill, she met a kind, gentle man, who was also a patient at the sanitarium. She dreamed of marrying him and having a little house "under the mountains." At her lowest ebb, her dream kept her going, and in 1948, they did marry. She then wrote a book about "all the good things life has brought me." *Wish I Might,* published in 1955, earned her enough in royalties to buy her mountain retreat.

A tragic life? Hardly! Isabel Smith achieved everything she set out to achieve, even when the odds against her were a thousand to one. Even flat on her back in bed she never quit growing, learning, and giving.

169

# A WELL-TRAINED MEMORY IS ONE THAT PERMITS YOU TO FORGET EVERYTHING THAT ISN'T WORTH REMEMBERING.

*Finally, brethren, whatsoever things are true, whatsoever things are honest, whatsoever things are just . . . if there be any virtue, and if there be any praise, think on these things.*
*Philippians 4:8*

According to an old legend, two monks named Tanzan and Ekido were traveling together down a muddy road one day. Heavy monsoon rains had saturated the area, and they were grateful for a few moments of sunshine to make their journey. Before long, they came around a bend and encountered a lovely girl in a silk kimono. She looked extremely forlorn as she stared at the muddy road before her.

At once, Tanzan responded to her plight. "Come here, girl," he said. Then lifting her in his arms, he carried her over the slippery ooze and set her down on the other side of the road.

Ekido didn't speak again to Tanzan. It was apparent to Tanzan that something was bothering him deeply, but try as he would, he couldn't get Ekido to talk to him. Then that night after they reached their intended lodging, Ekido could no longer restrain his anger and disappointment. "We monks don't go near females," he said to Tanzan in an accusing voice. "We especially don't go near young and lovely maidens. It is dangerous. Why did you do that?"

"I left the girl back there, Ekido," replied Tanzan. And then he asked the key question, "Are you still carrying her?"

Train your mind to think on pure things. Make a conscious decision to stop any thought that doesn't line up with the teachings of the Bible. Take those thoughts captive! (See 2 Corinthians 10:5.)

# DEFEAT IS NOT THE WORST OF FAILURES. NOT TO HAVE TRIED IS THE TRUE FAILURE.

*Be strong and of a good courage; be not afraid,
neither be thou dismayed: for the LORD thy
God is with thee withersoever thou goest.*
*Joshua 1:9*

There once was a young man who lived a most miserable life. Orphaned before he was three, he was taken in by strangers. He was kicked out of school, suffered from poverty, and as the result of inherited physical weaknesses, he developed serious heart trouble as a teenager. His beloved wife died early in their marriage. He lived as an invalid most of his adult life, and he eventually died at the young age of forty. By all outward appearances, he was defeated by life and doomed to be forgotten by history.

Even so, he never quit trying to express himself and to achieve success over the twenty years of his active work life. In that period, he produced some of the most brilliant articles, essays, and criticisms ever written. His poetry is still read widely and studied by virtually every high school student in the United States. His short stories and detective stories are famous. One of his poems, on display at the famous Huntington Library in California, has been valued at more than fifty thousand dollars, which is far more than the young man earned in his entire lifetime.

His name? Edgar Allan Poe.

Circumstances don't affect your chances for success nearly as much as your level of effort!

# UNLESS YOU TRY TO DO SOMETHING BEYOND WHAT YOU HAVE ALREADY MASTERED, YOU WILL NEVER GROW.

*Reaching forth unto those things which are before, I press toward the mark for the prize of the high calling of God in Christ Jesus.*
*Philippians 3:13-14*

# God's Little Devotional Book

After falling twice in the 1988 Olympic speed-skating races, Dan Jansen sought out sports psychologist Dr. Jim Loehr, who helped him find a new balance between sport and life, and who helped him pay more attention to the mental aspects of skating. Peter Mueller became his coach, putting him through workouts that Dan has since described as the "toughest I've ever known." By the time the 1994 Olympics arrived, Jansen had more confidence than ever. He had set a five-hundred-meter world record just two months before. That race seemed to be all his!

During the five-hundred-meter race, Jansen fell. He was shaken. Dr. Loehr immediately advised, "Start preparing for the one thousand. Put the five hundred behind you immediately. Stop reliving it." The one thousand! For years Dan had felt he could not win at that distance. He had always considered it his weaker event. Now it was his last chance for an Olympic medal. As the race began, Jansen said, "I just seemed to be sailing along," and then he slipped and came within an inch of stepping on a lane marker. Still, he didn't panic. He raced on and recorded a world-record time that won him the gold medal!

Once you reach a goal or master a skill, set your sights higher. As you approach each goal, set a new one. Don't be intimidated! Your toughest goal can become your greatest triumph.

CLASS OF 2000

175

# I DON'T KNOW THE SECRET TO SUCCESS, BUT THE KEY TO FAILURE IS TO TRY TO PLEASE EVERYONE.

*Am I now trying to win the*
*approval of men, or of God?*
*Galatians 1:10 NIV*

A young man once studied violin under a world-renowned violinist and master teacher. He worked hard for several years at perfecting his talent, and the day finally came when he was called upon to give his first major public recital in the large city where both he and his teacher lived. Following each selection, which he performed with great skill and passion, the performer seemed uneasy about the great applause he received. Even though he knew that those in the audience were musically astute and not likely to give such applause to a less than superior performance, the young man acted almost as if he couldn't hear the appreciation that was being showered upon him.

At the close of the last number, the applause was thunderous and numerous "Bravos" were shouted. But the talented young violinist had his eyes glued on one spot only. Finally, when an elderly man in the first row of the balcony smiled and nodded to him in approval, the young man relaxed and beamed with both relief and joy. His teacher had praised his work! The applause of thousands meant nothing until he had first won the approval of the master.

Who are you trying to please today? You will never be able to please everyone, but you can please the One Who matters most—your Father God. Keep your eyes on Him, and you can't fail.

# KITES RISE HIGHEST AGAINST THE WIND, NOT WITH IT.

*When the way is rough, your patience*
*has a chance to grow. So let it grow, and*
*don't try to squirm out of your problems.*
*James 1:3-4 TLB*

The engineers hired to build a suspension bridge across the Niagara River faced a serious problem: how to get the first cable from one side of the river to the next. The river was too wide to throw a cable across it and too swift to cross by boat.

An engineer finally came up with a solution! With a favoring stiff wind, a kite was lofted and allowed to drift over the river and land on the opposite shore. Attached to the kite was a very light string, which was threaded through the kite's tip so that both ends of the string were in the hands of the kite flyer. Once the kite was in the hand of engineers on the far side, they removed the kite from its string and set up a pulley. A small rope was attached to one end of the original kite string and pulled across the river. At the end of this string, a piece of rope was attached and pulled across and so on, until a cable strong enough to sustain the iron cable, which supported the bridge, could be drawn across the water.

Let your faith soar like that kite! Release it to God, believing that He can and will help you. When you link your released faith with patience and persistence, you will have what it takes to tackle virtually any problem.

# THE SECRET OF SUCCESS IS TO BE LIKE A DUCK— SMOOTH AND UNRUFFLED ON TOP, BUT PADDLING FURIOUSLY UNDERNEATH.

*I laboured more abundantly than they all:*
*yet not I, but the grace of God which was with me.*
*1 Corinthians 15:10*

Wallace E. Johnson, president of Holiday Inns and one of America's most successful builders, once said, "I always keep a card in my billfold with the following verses and refer to them frequently: *Ask and it shall be given you; seek and ye shall find; knock, and it shall be opened unto you: for everyone that asketh receiveth; and he that seeketh findeth; and to him that knocketh, it shall be opened (Matthew 7:7-8).*

"These verses are among God's greatest promises. Yet they are a little one-sided. They indicate a philosophy of receiving but not of giving. One day as my wife, Alma, and I were seeking God's guidance for a personal problem, I came across the following verse which has since been a daily reminder to me of what my responsibility as a businessman is to God: *Study to shew thyself approved unto God, a workman that needeth not to be ashamed, rightly dividing the word of truth (2 Timothy 2:15).*

"Since then I have measured my actions against the phrase: *A workman that needeth not to be ashamed.*"

FAITH ON THE INSIDE + WORKS ON THE OUTSIDE = A SUCCESSFUL LIFE!

# THE CHEERFUL MAN WILL DO MORE IN THE SAME TIME, WILL DO IT BETTER, WILL PRESERVE IT LONGER, THAN THE SAD OR SULLEN.

*When a man is gloomy, everything*
*seems to go wrong; when he is*
*cheerful, everything seems right!*
*Proverbs 15:15 TLB*

A little boy was once overheard talking to himself as he strutted out of his house into the backyard, carrying a baseball bat and ball. Once in the yard, he tipped his baseball cap to his eager puppy, and picking up the bat and ball, he announced with a loud voice, "I'm the greatest hitter in the world!"

He then proceeded to toss the ball into the air, swing at it, and miss. "Strike one!" he cried, as if playing the role of umpire.

He picked up the ball, threw it into the air, and said again, "I'm the greatest baseball hitter ever!" Again he swung at the ball and missed. "Strike two!" he announced to his dog and the yard.

Undaunted, he picked up the ball, examined his bat, and then just before tossing the ball into the air, announced once again, "I'm the greatest hitter who ever lived!" He swung the bat hard, but missed the ball for the third time. "Strike three!" he cried. Then he added, "Wow! What a pitcher! I'm the greatest pitcher in all the world!"

A positive mental attitude goes a long way toward making a difficult job seem small.

# MONEY IS A GOOD SERVANT BUT A BAD MASTER.

*The rich ruleth over the poor, and the borrower is servant to the lender.*
*Proverbs 22:7*

At the age of twenty-four, financial advisor and author Ron Blue felt he had everything he needed to be successful—an MBA degree, a CPA certificate, and a prestigious position in the New York City office of the world's largest CPA firm. But then at the age of thirty-two, he committed his life to Jesus Christ and began to see life from a new perspective. When he decided to establish his own financial advisory firm, he used his skills to develop a business plan and arrange for a ten-thousand-dollar line of credit at a bank. Almost immediately, however, he felt convicted that God did not want him to borrow money to start his business. He canceled the credit line, not knowing what to do next but knowing he was not to go into debt.

One day, while explaining his business idea to a friend, the friend said, "Would you consider designing a financial seminar for our executives who are getting ready to retire?" Ron jumped at the opportunity. His friend was the training director for a large company, and the company agreed to pay six thousand dollars in advance for development of the seminar, then one thousand dollars each for four seminars during the year. Ron had the ten thousand dollars he needed without borrowing a dime.

Do your best to stay out of debt. You'll feel much freer, and God will bless you for trusting in Him.

185

# NO PLAN IS WORTH THE PAPER IT IS PRINTED ON UNLESS IT STARTS YOU DOING SOMETHING.

*But be ye doers of the word, and not hearers only, deceiving your own selves.*
*James 1:22*

Nelson Diebel, a hyperactive and delinquent child, was enrolled in The Peddie School where he met swimming coach, Chris Martin, who believed the more one practices, the better one performs. Within a month, he had Nelson swimming thirty to forty hours a week, even though Nelson could not sit still in a classroom for fifteen minutes. Martin saw potential in Nelson. He constantly put new goals in front of the boy, trying to get him to focus and turn his anger into strength. Nelson eventually qualified for the Junior Nationals, and his fast times qualified him for Olympic Trials.

Then Nelson broke both hands and arms in a diving accident, and doctors warned he probably would never regain his winning form. Martin said to him, "You're coming all the way back . . . . If you're not committed to that, we're going to stop right now." Nelson agreed, and within weeks after his casts were off, he was swimming again.

In 1992, Nelson Diebel won an Olympic gold medal. As he accepted his medal, he recalls thinking: *I planned and dreamed and worked so hard and I did it!* The kid who once couldn't sit still and who had no ambition had learned to make a plan, pursue it, and achieve it. He had become a winner in far more than swimming!

Let your plans motivate you to start working toward your goals. Dream big dreams!

# LIFE IS A COIN. YOU CAN SPEND IT ANY WAY YOU WISH, BUT YOU CAN SPEND IT ONLY ONCE.

*It is appointed unto men once
to die, but after this the judgment.*
*Hebrews 9:27*

Frank, the head and founder of a major contracting firm, refused to celebrate the holidays, saying only, "Christmas is for children." Then one brisk December day, Frank was walking to work and was drawn to a Nativity scene in a department store window. He saw the Child anew. As he started to move away, a sign across the street caught his attention: "Holy Innocents Home." His mind raced back to a Sunday school lesson years ago about how King Herod had feared the Baby Jesus and slaughtered children in Bethlehem. He recalled the day his own son, David, had died at the age of eighteen months. He had not been able to speak his name since.

Impulsively, Frank visited the library and was surprised to learn that Herod's men were estimated to have killed twenty children. He left the library with a mission. Later that night, he told his wife, Adele, that he had visited the orphanage and that he had given money for the building of a new wing. Then he said, "They are going to name it for David." What Frank did not tell his wife was that he had had a vision of twenty children playing in a bright new wing at Holy Innocents. As Adele hugged him, the vision came again, but this time, there were twenty-one children at play.

Don't miss the opportunity to spend your life on something worthwhile. You may have several opportunities, some big and some small, but none of them will be insignificant.

# ONLY PASSIONS, GREAT PASSIONS, CAN ELEVATE THE SOUL TO GREAT THINGS.

*Fervent in spirit; serving the Lord.*
*Romans 12:11*

The German sculptor, Dannaker, worked for two years on a statue of Christ until it looked perfect to him. He called a little girl into his studio, and pointing to the statue, he asked her, "Who is that?" The little girl promptly replied, "A great man."

Dannaker was disheartened. He took his chisel and began anew. For six long years, he toiled. Again, he invited a little girl into his workshop, stood her before the figure, and said, "Who is that?" She looked up at it for a moment, and then tears welled up in her eyes as she folded her hands across her chest and said, *Suffer the little children to come unto me (Mark 10:14)*. This time Dannaker knew he had succeeded.

The sculptor later confessed that during those six years, Christ had revealed Himself to him in a vision, and he had only transferred to the marble what he had seen with his inner eyes.

Later, when Napoleon Bonaparte asked him to make a statue of Venus for the Louvre, Dannaker refused. "A man," he said, "who had seen Christ can never employ his gifts in carving a pagan goddess. My art is henceforth a consecrated thing."

The true value of a work comes not from effort, nor its completion, but from Christ who inspires it.

191

# FAILURES WANT PLEASING METHODS; SUCCESSES WANT PLEASING RESULTS.

*No discipline seems pleasant at the time,
but painful. Later on, however, it produces
a harvest of righteousness and peace
for those who have been trained by it.*
*Hebrews 12:11 NIV*

Sadie Delaney's father taught her always to strive to do better than her competition. She proved the value of that lesson shortly before she received her teaching license. A supervisor came to watch her and two other student teachers. Their assignment was to teach a class to bake cookies. Since the supervisor didn't have time for each teacher to go through the entire lesson, she divided the lesson, and Sadie was assigned to teach the girls how to serve and clean up.

The first student teacher panicked and forgot to halve the recipe and preheat the oven. The second girl was so behind because of the first girl's errors that the students made a mess in forming and baking the cookies. Then it was Sadie's turn. She said to the girls, "Listen, we have to work together as a team." They quickly baked the remaining dough. Several girls were lined up to scrub pans as soon as the cookies came out of the oven. Within ten minutes, they had several dozen perfect cookies and a clean kitchen. The supervisor was so impressed, she offered Sadie a substitute teacher's license on the spot. Sadie soon became the first black person ever to teach domestic science in New York City's public high schools.

Even when you have every right to blame others who have gone before you, don't make excuses. Do what it takes to get the job done!

---

.

God's Little Devotional Book

# ONCE A WORD HAS BEEN ALLOWED TO ESCAPE, IT CANNOT BE RECALLED.

*Let no corrupt communication proceed out of your mouth, but that which is good to the use of edifying, that it may minister grace unto the hearers.*
*Ephesians 4:29*

194

A man once sat down to have dinner with his family. Before they began to eat, the family members joined hands around the table, and the man said a prayer, thanking God for the food, the hands that had prepared it, and for the source of all life. During the meal, however, he complained at length about the staleness of the bread, the bitterness of the coffee, and a bit of mold he found on one edge of the brick of cheese.

His young daughter asked him, "Daddy, do you think God heard you say grace before the meal?"

"Of course, honey," he answered confidently.

Then she asked, "Do you think God heard everything that was said during dinner?" The man answered, "Why, yes, I believe so. God hears everything."

She thought for a moment and then asked, "Daddy, which do you think God believed?"

The Lord hears everything we say during a day, not only those words that are addressed specifically to Him. Once you've said something, you can't take it back. Would you mind if God listened in on your conversations?

MOST OF THE THINGS WORTH DOING IN THE WORLD HAD BEEN DECLARED IMPOSSIBLE BEFORE THEY WERE DONE.

*With God all things are possible.*
*Matthew 19:26*

196

Consider these examples of resistance to ideas and inventions that we now consider commonplace:

1. In Germany, "experts" proved that if trains went as fast as fifteen miles an hour—considered a frightful speed—blood would spurt from the travelers' noses and passengers would suffocate when going through tunnels. In the United States, experts said the introduction of the railroad would require the building of many insane asylums since people would be driven mad with terror at the sight of the locomotives.

2. The New York ywca announced typing lessons for women in 1881 and vigorous protest erupted on the grounds that the female constitution would break down under the strain.

3. When the idea of iron ships was proposed, experts insisted that they would not float, would damage more easily than wooden ships when grounding, that it would be difficult to preserve the iron bottom from rust, and that iron would play havoc with compass readings.

4. New Jersey farmers resisted the first successful cast-iron plow invented in 1797, claiming that the cast iron would poison the land and stimulate the growth of weeds.

Don't let the word "impossible" stop you. If inventors and visionaries left every "impossible" task undone, our lives would be considerably more difficult. Nothing worth doing is impossible with the help of God!

197

# OBSTACLES ARE THOSE FRIGHTFUL THINGS YOU SEE WHEN YOU TAKE YOUR EYES OFF THE GOAL.

*So Peter . . . walked on the water toward Jesus.*
*But when he looked around at the high waves,*
*he was terrified and began to sink.*
*Matthew 14:29-30 TLB*

During the darkest days of the Civil War, the hopes of the Union nearly died. When certain goals seemed unreachable, the leaders of the Union turned to President Abraham Lincoln for solace, guidance, and encouragement. Once when a delegation called at the White House and detailed a long list of crises facing the nation, Lincoln told this story:

"Years ago a young friend and I were out one night when a shower of meteors fell from the clear November sky. The young man was frightened, but I told him to look up in the sky past the shooting stars to the fixed stars beyond, shining serene in the firmament, and I said, 'Let us not mind the meteors, but let us keep our eyes on the stars.'"

When times are troubled or life seems to be changing too fast, keep your inner eyes of faith and hope on those things that you know to be lasting and sure. Don't limit your gaze to what you know or who you know, but focus on Whom you know. God alone—and a relationship with Him that is eternal—is the Supreme Goal. He never changes, and He cannot be removed from His place as the King of Glory.

# A GOOD REPUTATION IS MORE VALUABLE THAN MONEY.

*A good name is rather to be*
*chosen than great riches.*
*Proverbs 22:1*

In *Up from Slavery,* Booker T. Washington describes meeting an ex-slave from Virginia:

"I found that this man had made a contract with his master, two or three years previous to the Emancipation Proclamation, to the effect that the slave was to be permitted to buy himself, by paying so much per year for his body; and while he was paying for himself, he was to be permitted to labor where and for whom he pleased.

"Finding that he could secure better wages in Ohio, he went there. When freedom came, he was still in debt to his master some 300 dollars. Notwithstanding that the Emancipation Proclamation freed him from any obligation to his master, this black man walked the greater portion of the distance back to where his old master lived in Virginia, and placed the last dollar, with interest, in his hands.

"In talking to me about this, the man told me that he knew that he did not have to pay his debt, but that he had given his word to his master, and his word he had never broken. He felt that he could not enjoy his freedom till he had fulfilled his promise."

Your ability to keep your word, not your ability to acquire money, is your true measure as a person!

# AN ERROR DOESN'T BECOME A MISTAKE UNTIL YOU REFUSE TO CORRECT IT.

*He who heeds discipline shows the way to life, but whoever ignores correction leads others astray.*
*Proverbs 10:17 NIV*

A janitor at the First Security Bank in Boise, Idaho, once accidentally put a box of eight thousand checks worth eight hundred and forty thousand dollars on a trash table. That night, the operator of the paper shredder dutifully dumped the box of checks into his machine, which cut the checks into quarter-inch shreds. He then dumped the paper scraps into a garbage can outside the bank. When the bank supervisor realized what happened the next morning, he wanted to cry.

Most of the checks had been cashed at the bank and were awaiting shipment to a clearinghouse. Their loss represented a bookkeeping nightmare since most of the checks were still unrecorded, and as a result, the bankers could not know who paid what to whom.

What did the supervisor do? He ordered that the shredded pieces be reconstructed. So fifty employees worked in two shifts for six hours a day inside six rooms—shifting, matching, and pasting the pieces together as if they were jigsaw puzzles—until all eight thousand of the checks were put together again.

Humpty Dumpty may have fallen from the wall. But did the king's men even try to put him together again? If you make a mistake, work on a solution!

203

# HATING PEOPLE IS LIKE BURNING DOWN YOUR OWN HOUSE TO GET RID OF A RAT.

*If ye bite and devour one another, take heed*
*that ye be not consumed one of another.*
*Galatians 5:15*

After two years in the navy, Willard Scott returned to his old job with NBC radio, but to a new supervisor. Willard found himself at odds with his new boss at every turn, and he was furious when he rescheduled "Joy Boys," a comedy show Willard did with Eddie Walker, for the worst slot on radio—eight to midnight. Willard was braced for a change-or-I'll-leave confrontation when he recalled Proverbs 19:11—*A man's wisdom gives him patience; it is to his glory to overlook an offense.* NIV. He and Eddie decided to work themselves to the bone, and within three years, they made "Joy Boys" the top-rated show in Washington.

Willard says, "I learned that I, too, had been wrong. In all my dealings with my boss, I had aggravated the problem. I knew he didn't like me, and in response I was barely civil to him and dodged him as much as I could. But one day he invited me to a station party I couldn't avoid. There I met his fiancé. She was bright, alive, and down-to-earth. *How could a woman like that care for anybody who didn't have something to recommend him?* I was able to get new insight into my boss' character. As time went on my attitude changed, and so did his." Willard and his boss became friends, and he remained at NBC.

Is there someone with whom you are at odds? If you're looking for the negative qualities in a person, you're sure to find them. Try seeing them with new eyes. A fresh perspective can change everything.

# LAUGHTER IS THE SUN THAT DRIVES WINTER FROM THE HUMAN FACE.

*A merry heart maketh a cheerful countenance:*
*but by sorrow of the heart the spirit is broken.*
*Proverbs 15:13*

# God's Little Devotional Book

A missionary from Sweden was once urged by his friends to give up his idea of returning to India because it was so hot there. "Man," the fellow Swede urged, as if telling his friend something he didn't already know, "it's 120 degrees in the shade in that country!" The Swedish missionary replied "Vell, ve don't alvays have to stay in the shade do ve?"

Humor is not a sin. It is a God-given escape hatch. Being able to see the lighter side of life is a virtue. Every vocation and circumstance of life has a lighter side, if we are only willing to see it. Wholesome humor can do a great deal to help defuse a tense, heated situation. In developing a good sense of humor, we must be able to laugh at our own mistakes; accept justified criticism and recover from it; and learn to avoid using statements that are unsuitable, even though they may be funny.

James M. Gray and William Houghton—two godly men—were praying together one day, and the elderly Dr. Gray concluded his prayer by saying, "Lord, keep me cheerful. Keep me from becoming a cranky, old man."

Keeping a sense of humor is a great way to become a sweet, patient, and encouraging person. Learn to laugh at yourself occasionally!

207

# GOOD NATURE BEGETS SMILES, SMILES BEGET FRIENDS, AND FRIENDS ARE BETTER THAN A FORTUNE.

*The light in the eyes [of him whose heart is joyful] rejoices the heart of others.*
Proverbs 15:30 AMP

It has been estimated that more than ninety-five percent of all Americans receive at least one or more Christmas cards each year. The average is actually more than seventy cards per family! Millions of cards are mailed worldwide each holiday season. Have you ever wondered where this custom began?

A museum director in the mid-nineteenth century had a personal habit of sending notes to his friends at Christmastime each year, just to wish them a joyful holiday season. One year, he found he had little time to write, and yet he still wanted to send a message of good cheer. He asked his friend, John Horsely, to design a card that he might sign and send. Those who received the cards loved them so much they created cards of their own. Thus the Christmas card was invented!

It's often the simple heartfelt gestures in life that speak most loudly of friendship. Ask yourself today, *What can I do to bring a smile to the face of a friend? What can I do to bring good cheer into the life of someone who is in need, trouble, sickness, or sorrow?* Follow-through on your answer. It's not a gift you are giving as much as a friendship you are building!

# NO PERSON WAS EVER HONORED FOR WHAT HE RECEIVED. HONOR HAS BEEN THE REWARD FOR WHAT HE GAVE.

*The righteous give without sparing.*
*Proverbs 21:26 NIV*

This American received a medical degree from New York University College of Medicine. He received an appointment to the Virus Research Laboratory at the University of Pittsburgh. He received an assignment from the army to develop a vaccine against influenza, and among the many honors he received was a Presidential Medal of Freedom.

However, Jonas Salk is not known for what he received, but for what he gave. He and his team of researchers gave their efforts to prepare an inactivated polio virus that could serve as an immunizing agent against polio. By 1952, they had created a vaccine, and in 1955, the vaccine was released for widespread use in the United States, virtually ending the ravaging, crippling effects of polio.

You will receive many opportunities in your life, and most likely, a number of certificates, diplomas, and awards. But what ultimately will count is what you do with the training you have received and the skills and traits you have developed.

Find a way to give, create, or generate something today that will benefit others. In your actions will be not only a potential for fame and reward, but also great personal satisfaction—the reward of highest value.

211

# THE DIFFERENCE BETWEEN THE RIGHT WORD AND THE ALMOST RIGHT WORD IS THE DIFFERENCE BETWEEN LIGHTNING AND THE LIGHTNING BUG.

*A word fitly spoken is like apples
of gold in pictures of silver.*
*Proverbs 25:11*

Consider the infamous statements listed below, and notice as you read that they all could be corrected by changing or inserting only one word!

"Everything that can be invented has been invented."—Charles H. Duell, U.S. Patent Office direct, 1899

"Who wants to hear actors talk?"—H.M. Warner, Warner Brothers Pictures 1927

"Sensible and responsible women do not want to vote."—Grover Cleveland, 1905

"There is no likelihood man can ever tap the power of the atom."—Robert Millikan, Nobel Prize winner in physics, 1923

"Heavier-than-air flying machines are impossible."—Lord Kelvin, president, Royal Society, 1895

"[Babe] Ruth made a big mistake when he gave up pitching."—Tris Speaker, 1927

*Gone with the Wind* is going to be the biggest flop in Hollywood history."—Gary Cooper

Isn't it amazing what a difference a word or two can make! Choose your words carefully. Always think before you speak.

213

# THIS WORLD BELONGS TO THE MAN WHO IS WISE ENOUGH TO CHANGE HIS MIND IN THE PRESENCE OF FACTS.

*Whoever heeds correction gains understanding.*
**Proverbs 15:32** NIV

214

A feud developed between two families who lived side by side in the mountains of Kentucky. It started when Grandpa Smith's cow jumped a stone fence and ate Grandpa Brown's corn. Brown shot the cow. A Smith boy then shot two Brown boys. The Browns shot one Smith. Bill Brown planned to kill a second Smith, but before he could, he was called away to war. While he was away, Bill's mother had a hard time making ends meet for her family, since Bill's father had been one of the victims.

At Christmas, the head of the Smith clan took his family to church. Usually he stayed outside, but this year it was so cold he went in to wait. The sermon was on Christ, the Prince of peace, who died in *our* place for *our* sins. It struck him hard. He realized what a crime he had committed, repented, and then secretly hired a young boy to carry a basket of food to the Brown's home every day until Bill returned.

Once home, Bill set out to discover who had so generously helped his family. He followed the boy to the Smith's house, where Smith met him and said, "Shoot me, Bill, if you want to. But Christ has already died for my sins, and I hope you'll forgive me, too." Bill did, and neighbors truly became neighbors again.

Never reach the point in life where you think you can't learn something new, or change your opinion about something. You are never too old, or too young, to be forgiven.

# DO NOT REMOVE A FLY FROM YOUR FRIEND'S FOREHEAD WITH A HATCHET.

*Reprove, rebuke, exhort, with*
*great patience and instruction.*
*2 Timothy 4:2 NASB*

216

One day, a young altar boy was serving the priest at a Sunday Mass being held in the country church of his small village. The boy, nervous in his new role at the altar, accidentally dropped the cruet of wine. The village priest immediately struck the boy sharply on the cheek, and in a very gruff voice, shouted so that many people could hear, "Leave the altar and don't come back!" That boy became Tito, the Communist leader who ruled Yugoslavia for many decades.

One day in a large city cathedral, a young boy was serving a bishop at a Sunday Mass. He, too, accidentally dropped the cruet of wine. The bishop turned to him, but rather than responding in anger, gently whispered with a warm twinkle in his eyes, "Someday you will be a priest." That boy grew up to become Archbishop Fulton Sheen.

Words have power. The childhood phrase, "Sticks and stones can break my bones, but words can never hurt me," simply isn't true. Words do hurt. They wound—sometimes deeply.

But words also can reward, build self-esteem, create friendships, give hope, and render a blessing. Words can heal and drive accomplishment.

Watch what you say to a friend today! Are your words like poison to the heart, or do they drip with the sweetness of honey?

# EVERY CALLING IS GREAT WHEN GREATLY PURSUED.

*I press toward the mark for the prize
of the high calling of God in Christ Jesus.*
*Philippians 3:14*

A farmer once caught a young eagle in the forest, brought it home, and raised it among his ducks and turkeys. Five years later, a naturalist came to visit him and saw the bird. "That's an eagle, not a chicken!" he said. "Yes," said the farmer, "but I've raised it to be a chicken." "Still," said the naturalist, "it has a wing span of fifteen feet. It's an eagle!" "It will never fly," said the farmer. The naturalist disagreed, and they decided to put their argument to the test.

First, the naturalist picked up the eagle and said, "Eagle, thou art an eagle; thou dost belong to the sky and not to this earth; stretch forth thy wings and fly." The eagle saw the chickens and jumped down. The next day, the naturalist took the eagle to the top of the house and said the same thing before letting the eagle go. Again, it spotted the chickens below and fluttered down to join them in feeding.

"One more try," said the naturalist. He took the eagle up a mountain. The trembling bird looked around, and then the naturalist made it look into the sun. Suddenly, the eagle stretched out its wings, gave a mighty screech, and flew away, never to return.

People may say you are just a hunk of flesh—a chicken rather than an eagle. But deep inside, you have a spirit created in God's image, and you are destined to fly.

# A GREAT MAN IS ALWAYS WILLING TO BE LITTLE.

*"But the greatest among you
shall be your servant."*
*Matthew 23:11 NASB*

220

Shortly after Booker T. Washington became head of the Tuskegee Institute in Alabama, he was walking past the house of a wealthy family. The woman of the house, assuming Washington was one of the yard workers her husband had hired, asked him if he would chop some wood for her. Professor Washington smiled, nodded, took off his coat, and chopped the wood. When he carried the armload of wood into the woman's kitchen, a servant girl recognized him and rushed to her mistress to tell her of his identity.

The next morning, the woman appeared in Washington's office. Apologizing profusely, she said repeatedly, "I did not know it was you I put to work."

Washington replied with generosity, "It's entirely all right, madam. I like to work and I'm delighted to do favors for my friends."

The woman was so taken with his manner and his willingness to forgive that she gave generous gifts to the institute, and persuaded many of her wealthy acquaintances to do likewise. In the end, Washington raised as much money for the institute from this one act of chopping wood as he did from any other fund-raising event!

A great leader is never beyond hard work. The willingness to serve others is the essence of true leadership.

221

# 'TIS BETTER TO BE ALONE, THAN IN BAD COMPANY.

*Do not be misled: "Bad company*
*corrupts good character."*
*1 Corinthians 15:33 NIV*

Coach Gregory watched with pride as Rashaan Salaam accepted the Heisman Trophy. He recalled the hotshot eighteen-year-old who, finally free from his mother's tight discipline, had arrived in Colorado ready to devour the world. He said, "Rashaan was a gangster wannabe. He came here wearing all this red stuff, talking about gangs. He hadn't done it back home because his mother would never have tolerated it." And neither did Gregory. He never lectured or preached to Rashaan, but he did ask him questions. When Rashaan came to him talking about his new friends, Gregory said, "Sure, they are your friends, but are you their friend? They know what you're trying to accomplish. They know the potential you have to do great things. If you are their friend, when they get ready to get into something, they'll say, 'Salaam, get out of here. Go home and study.'"

As a coach, Gregory wanted Salaam to "find daylight" and get into the end zone, but as his friend, he wanted him to live in the daylight and make it to life's goal line as a productive citizen. Winning a football game is never a one-man effort. It's a team effort. The same holds true for life, and the good news is you can choose the players on your team!

CLASS OF 2000

223

# THE ROTTEN APPLE SPOILS HIS COMPANION.

*He that walketh with wise men shall be wise:*
*but a companion of fools shall be destroyed.*
*Proverbs 13:20*

In his book *The Mind of Watergate,* psychiatrist Leo Rangell, m.d., relates what he calls a "compromise of integrity" as he analyzes the relationship between former President Richard M. Nixon and several of his closest confidants. He records a conversation between investigative committee member Senator Howard Baker and young Herbert L. Porter:

*Baker:* "Did you ever have any qualms about what you were doing? Did you ever think of saying, 'I do not think this is quite right.' Did you ever think of that?"

*Porter:* "Yes, I did."

*Baker:* "What did you do about it?"

*Porter:* "I did not do anything."

*Baker:* "Why didn't you?"

*Porter:* "In all honesty, probably because of the fear of the group pressure that would ensue, of not being a team player."

There's nothing wrong with being a team player, as long as you choose the right team! You will become like your friends, even as they change and become a little more like you. Therefore, choose your friends cautiously and thoughtfully.

# PATIENCE IS BITTER BUT ITS FRUIT IS SWEET.

*For ye have need of patience, that, after ye have done the will of God, ye might receive the promise.*
*Hebrews 10:36*

We often think of great artists and musicians as having "bursts" of genius. More often, they are models of painstaking patience. Their greatest works tend to have been accomplished over long periods and in extreme hardships.

Beethoven is said to have rewritten each bar of his music at least a dozen times.

Josef Haydn produced more than eight hundred musical compositions before writing *The Creation,* the oratorio for which he is most famous.

Michelangelo's *Last Judgment* is considered one of the twelve master paintings of the ages. It took him eight years to complete. He produced more than two thousand sketches and renderings in the process.

Leonardo da Vinci worked on *The Last Supper* for ten years, often working so diligently that he forgot to eat.

When he was quite elderly, the pianist Ignace Paderewski was asked by an admirer, "Is it true that you still practice every day?" He replied, "Yes, at least six hours a day." The admirer said in awe, "You must have a world of patience." Paderewski said, "I have no more patience than the next fellow. I just use mine."

Put your patience to use in the pursuit of your dreams.

227

# MOTIVATION IS WHEN YOUR DREAMS PUT ON WORK CLOTHES.

*Whatever you do, work at it with all your heart,*
*as working for the Lord, not for men.*
*Colossians 3:23 NIV*

In 1972, *Life* magazine published a story about the amazing adventures of John Goddard. When he was fifteen, John's grandmother said, "If only I had done that when I was young. . . . " Determined not to make that statement at the end of his life, John wrote out one hundred and twenty seven goals for his life.

He named ten rivers he wanted to explore and seventeen mountains he wanted to climb. He set goals of becoming an Eagle Scout, a world traveler, and a pilot. Also on his list was: ride a horse in the Rose Bowl parade, dive in a submarine, retrace the travels of Marco Polo, read the Bible from cover to cover, and read the entire *Encyclopedia Britannica*.

He also planned to read the entire works of Shakespeare, Plato, Dickens, Socrates, Aristotle, and several other classic authors. He desired to learn to play the flute and violin, marry, have children (he had five), pursue a career in medicine, and serve as a missionary for his church.

Sound impossible? At the age of forty-seven, John Goddard had accomplished one hundred and three of his goals!

Your list of goals may not be as extensive as John Goddard's, but if you don't have *some* goals in life, you'll find that you have little motivation to get up in the morning and little satisfaction as your head hits the pillow each night.

# NOT ONLY TO SAY THE RIGHT THING IN THE RIGHT PLACE, BUT FAR MORE DIFFICULT, TO LEAVE UNSAID THE WRONG THING AT THE TEMPTING MOMENT.

*Self-control means controlling the tongue!*
*A quick retort can ruin everything.*
*Proverbs 13:3 TLB*

William Penn, founding leader of the colony that became Pennsylvania, had these rules for conversation: "Avoid company where it is not profitable or necessary, and in those occasions, speak little, and last. Silence is wisdom where speaking is folly, and always safe. Some are so foolish as to interrupt and anticipate those that speak instead of hearing and thinking before they answer, which is uncivil, as well as silly. If thou thinkest twice before thou speakest once, thou wilt speak twice the better for it. Better to say nothing than not to the purpose. And to speak pertinently, consider both what is fit, and when it is fit, to speak. In all debates, let truth be thy aim, not victory or an unjust interest; and endeavor to gain, rather than to expose, thy antagonist."

A little girl named Mary had come home from a tough day at school. She stretched herself out on the living room sofa to have her own private pity party. She moaned to her mother and brother, "Nobody loves me . . . the whole world hates me!"

Her brother, busily occupied with his Nintendo, hardly looked her way as he passed on this encouraging word: "That's not true, Mary. Some people don't even know you."

Mary, no doubt, was not amused. She probably wished her brother had heeded the advice of William Penn. One of the greatest skills you can develop in life is the ability to control your tongue!

231

# SCHOOL SEEKS TO GET YOU READY FOR EXAMINATION; LIFE GIVES THE FINALS.

*Examine yourselves to see whether you are in the faith; test yourselves.*
2 Corinthians 13:5 NIV

232

The Koh-in-noor diamond is among the world's most spectacular. It is part of the British crown jewels, presented to Queen Victoria by a maharajah in India when the maharajah was only a young boy.

Years later, when he was a grown man, the maharajah visited Queen Victoria in England. He asked that the stone be brought from the Tower of London, where it was kept in safety, to Buckingham Palace. The queen did as he requested.

Taking the diamond in his hand, he knelt before the queen and presented it back to her, saying, "Your Majesty, I gave this jewel when I was a child, too young to know what I was doing. I want to give it to you again in the fullness of my strength, with all of my heart and affection, and gratitude, now and forever, fully realizing all that I do."

A day will come when you likely will look back and say, "I'm grateful for my teachers, and the lessons they taught me about discipline, concentration, hard work, cooperation, and the right and wrong ways to compete." Even more valuable will be the day when you look in a mirror and say, "Knowing what I now know about life, I see value in continuing to teach these lessons to myself."

233

# DILIGENCE IS THE MOTHER OF GOOD FORTUNE.

*The plans of the diligent lead to profit.*

Proverbs 21:5 *NIV*

The *Sixty-four Thousand-Dollar Question* was the hottest show on television in 1955. The more Joyce watched the program, the more she thought, "I could do that." At the time, Joyce had quit her teaching job to raise her daughter, and she and her husband were living on fifty dollars a month. She never dreamed of winning the top prize—*any* prize at that point would have helped greatly.

As a psychologist by training, Joyce analyzed the show. She saw that each contestant had a built-in incongruity—the marine who was a gourmet cook, the shoemaker who knew about opera. She looked at herself. She was a short, blond psychologist and mother with no incongruity. After some thought, she decided to become an expert in boxing! She ate, drank, and slept boxing, studying its statistics, personalities, and history. When she felt she was ready, she applied as a contestant for the show, was accepted, won, and won again, until she eventually won the sixty four thousand dollar prize.

That experience led her to dream of a career as a television journalist who might translate the results of psychological research into terms that people could use in their everyday lives. Once she saw that possibility, there was no stopping Dr. Joyce Brothers.

True success never comes by chance. Diligently apply yourself to your goals, and your dreams will come true.

235

# THE ROAD TO SUCCESS IS DOTTED WITH MANY TEMPTING PARKING PLACES.

*Let us lay aside every weight, and the sin
which doth so easily beset us, and let us run
with patience the race that is set before us.*
*Hebrews 12:1*

The first thing to emerge at a baby giraffe's birth is its front hooves and head. Minutes later, the newborn is hurled from its mother's body, falls ten feet, and lands on its back. Within seconds, it rolls to an upright position with its legs tucked under its body. From this position, it views the world for the first time and shakes off any remaining birthing fluid.

The mother giraffe lowers her head just long enough to take a quick look at her calf, and then she does what seems to be a very unreasonable thing—she kicks her baby, sending it sprawling head over heels. If it doesn't get up, she kicks it again and again until the calf finally stands on its wobbly legs. Then what does the mother giraffe do? She kicks it off its feet! Why? She wants it to remember how to get up.

In the wild, baby giraffes must be able to get up as quickly as possible to stay with the herd and avoid becoming a meal for lions, hyenas, leopards, or wild hunting dogs. The best way a mother giraffe has of ensuring that her calf lives is for her to teach it to get up quickly and get with it.

Don't complain if those who love you push you into action when you'd rather be in "park." They are doing you a favor.

237

# WHEN YOU ARE LABORING FOR OTHERS LET IT BE WITH THE SAME ZEAL AS IF IT WERE FOR YOURSELF.

*Each of you should look not only to your own
interests, but also to the interests of others.*
*Philippians 2:4 NIV*

On May 21, 1946, a scientist at Los Alamos was carrying out a necessary experiment in preparation for an atomic test to be conducted in the waters of the South Pacific. He had successfully performed this experiment many times before. It involved pushing two hemispheres of uranium together to determine the amount of U-235 needed for a chain reaction—the amount scientists call "a critical mass." Just as the mass became critical, he would push the hemispheres apart with his screwdriver, instantly stopping the chain reaction.

That day, however, just as the material became critical, the screwdriver slipped. The hemispheres of uranium came too close together, and instantly, the room was filled with a dazzling bluish haze. Young Louis Soltin, instead of ducking and thereby possibly saving himself, tore the two hemispheres apart with his hands, thus interrupting the chain reaction.

In this instant, self-forgetful act, he saved the lives of seven other people who were in the room. He, however, died in agony nine days later.

Today, do something for someone else with the same energy you would use if you were doing it for yourself.

239

THE BIBLE KNOWS
NOTHING OF A
HIERARCHY OF
LABOR. NO WORK
IS DEGRADING.
IT IF OUGHT TO
BE DONE, THEN IT
IS GOOD WORK.

*To rejoice in his labour; this is the gift of God.*
*Ecclesiastes 5:19*

When David was twelve, he convinced a restaurant manager that he was actually sixteen and was hired as a lunch-counter waiter for twenty-five cents an hour. The place was owned by two Greek immigrant brothers, Frank and George, who had started their lives in America as a dishwasher and hot-dog seller. David remembers that they set high standards and never asked anything of their employees that they wouldn't do themselves. Frank once told David, "As long as you try, you can always work for me. But when you don't try, you can't work for me." Trying meant everything from working hard to treating customers politely. Once, when Frank noticed a waitress giving a customer a rough time he fired her on the spot and waited on the table himself. David determined that would never happen to him.

The usual tip for waiters in those days was a dime, but David discovered that if he brought the food out quickly and was especially polite, he sometimes got a quarter as a tip. He set a goal for himself to see how many customers he could wait on in one night. His record was one hundred!

Today, R. David Thomas is better known as "Dave," the founder and senior chairman of Wendy's International, Inc., a chain of forty three hundred restaurants.

No matter what job you do, do it well. The Bible tells us to do all our work *as unto the Lord. (Colossians 3:23.)*

241

# THE RIPEST PEACH IS HIGHEST ON THE TREE.

*Let us not become weary in doing good,*
*for at the proper time we will reap*
*a harvest if we do not give up.*
*Galatians 6:9 NIV*

McCormick's father was what many might call a "tinkerer." A mechanical genius, he invented many farm devices. Sadly, however, he became the laughingstock of his community for attempting to make a grain-cutting device. For years, he worked on the project but never succeeded in getting it to operate reliably.

In spite of the discouragement his father experienced and the continuing ridicule of neighbors, young McCormick took up the old machine as his own project. He also experienced years of experimentation and failure. Then one day, he succeeded in constructing a reaper that would harvest grain.

Even so, jealous opposition prevented the invention from being used for a number of years. McCormick was able to make sales only after he gave a personal guarantee to each purchaser that the reaper would do the job he claimed it could do. Finally, after decades of trial and error, hoping and waiting, a firm in Cincinnati agreed to manufacture one hundred machines, and the famous McCormick reaper was "born."

To get to the ripest peach on the highest branch, you need to climb one limb at a time, and not be defeated by the scrape of bark, the occasional fall, and the frequent feeling of being left dangling!

243

WHEN YOU DO THE
THINGS YOU HAVE TO
DO WHEN YOU HAVE
TO DO THEM, THE DAY
WILL COME WHEN
YOU CAN DO THE
THINGS YOU WANT
TO DO WHEN YOU
WANT TO DO THEM.

*He becometh poor that dealeth with a slack hand:*
*but the hand of the diligent maketh rich.*
*Proverbs 10:4*

The bee is often described as being "busy." It deserves this adjective! To produce one pound of honey, a bee must visit fifty six thousand clover heads. Since each head has sixty flower tubes, a bee must make a total of three million, three hundred sixty thousand visits. In the process, the average bee would travel the equivalent of three times around the world.

To make just one *tablespoon* of honey, the amount that might go on a biscuit, a little bee must make forty two hundred trips to the flowers, averaging about ten trips a day, each trip lasting approximately twenty minutes. It visits four hundred different flowers.

Day in, day out, the work of a bee is fairly unglamorous. It flies, it takes in nectar, it flies some more, and it deposits nectar. But in the process, it produces, and what it produces creates a place for it in the hive.

You may think your daily chores are a waste of time. But in fact, your completion of those chores is "making" you. One day, you won't even have to think: *I must get disciplined. I must get to work. I must stick with it.* If you have done your chores faithfully and to the best of your ability, the chores will have become a part of the way you tackle every challenge the rest of your life.

245

# A MAN WITHOUT MIRTH IS LIKE A WAGON WITHOUT SPRINGS, HE IS JOLTED DISAGREEABLY BY EVERY PEBBLE IN THE ROAD.

*A merry heart doeth good like a medicine:*
*but a broken spirit drieth the bones.*
*Proverbs 17:22*

D r. Ashley Montagu met two young men shortly after the end of World War II. They had spent two years in Auschwitz, the cruel death camp operated by the Nazis. Prior to Auschwitz, they had lived in Vienna in a cellar where they had been kept hidden by Christian friends. All of the others housed with them in the cellar had been exterminated solely because they were Jews. After the war ended, these two men had walked from Vienna to Berlin, hoping to find relatives. There, they were picked up by an American Jewish soldier who brought them to America. Both of them wanted to become physicians and that's how Dr. Montagu, a professor in a medical school, came to meet them. Noting that they "didn't exhibit any of the scars that one might have expected from their unhappy existence," he asked them how they came to be such cheerful people.

They replied, "A group of us decided that no matter what happened, it wouldn't get us down." They told him they had attempted to be cheerful regardless of their circumstances, never yielding for a moment to the idea that they were either inferior or doomed.

They were living proof to Dr. Montagu that even under impossible conditions, it's possible to be happy!

247

# THE TWO MOST IMPORTANT WORDS: "THANK YOU." THE MOST IMPORTANT WORD: "WE." THE LEAST IMPORTANT WORD: "I."

*Don't be selfish. . . . Be humble,*
*thinking of others as better than yourself.*
*Philippians 2:3 TLB*

There's an old saying that goes, "It needs more skill than I can tell, to play the second fiddle well."

Along that line, Leonard Bernstein was once asked which instrument was the most difficult to play. He thought for a moment and said, "The second fiddle. I can get plenty of first violinists, but to find someone who can play the second fiddle with enthusiasm—that's a problem. And if we have no second fiddle, we have no harmony."

General Robert E. Lee was a man who knew the value of playing second fiddle. This great general never stopped being a true southern gentleman. Once, while riding on a train to Richmond, he was seated at the rear of the car. All the other places were filled with officers and soldiers. A poorly dressed, elderly woman boarded the coach at a rural station, and finding no seat offered to her, she trudged down the aisle toward the back of the car. Immediately, Lee stood up and offered her his place. One after another of the men then arose and offered the general his seat. "No, gentlemen," he replied, "if there is none for this lady, there can be none for me!"

Genuine humility is what prompts us to offer a heartfelt thank you and to favor others over ourselves.

249

# HERE'S THE KEY TO SUCCESS AND THE KEY TO FAILURE: WE BECOME WHAT WE THINK ABOUT.

*Finally, brethren, whatsoever things are true, whatsoever things are honest . . . if there be any virtue, and if there be any praise, think on these things.*
*Philippians 4:8*

A number of years ago the John Hancock Mutual Life Insurance Company ran an ad that said:

"There was once a man who loved nature with such a deep and moving love that she told him one of her secrets. She gave him the power to create new plants. The man, whose name was Luther Burbank . . . saw that every plant was a child. It had its own face, own promise, its unique touch of genius or character. And if that promise were tended and encouraged, the plant would grow more useful and beautiful each year. Luther Burbank . . . made potatoes grow larger, whiter, more delicious than they had ever been. He taught the cactus of the desert to throw away its spines, so that cattle could fatten upon it, and made the blackberry shed its thorns, so it would not cut the fingers of the pickers. For him, the plum grew without pits, and strawberries ripened all year . . . he left the earth covered with flowers and fruits that no one had ever attempted to grow before. And all because he knew a secret. He knew that everything that lives has the power to become greater."

Choose to see new possibilities. Put your mind to them. Let them be the focus of your thoughts, and then pursue them! You will become greater for it.

251

# ALWAYS BEAR IN MIND THAT YOUR OWN RESOLUTION TO SUCCESS IS MORE IMPORTANT THAN ANY OTHER ONE THING.

*For the LORD God will help me; therefore shall I not be confounded: therefore have I set my face like a flint, and I know that I shall not be ashamed.*
*Isaiah 50:7*

Famous stage and film actress Helen Hayes believed her "resoluteness" about her own potential for success played an important role at the beginning of her career. She once told the story of a particular audition: "Before the authors gave me the script, they observed, in a matter-of-course manner, 'Of course you play piano? You'll have to sing to your own accompaniment in the piece.' As these alarming tidings were in the course of being made, I caught a bewildered look in my mother's eyes, and so I spoke up before she could. 'Certainly I play piano,' I answered.

"As we left the theater, my mother sighed, 'I hate to see you start under a handicap,' she said. 'What made you say you could play piano?' 'The feeling that I will play before rehearsals begin,' I said. We went at once to try to rent a piano and ended by buying one. I began lessons at once, practiced finger exercises till I could no longer see the notes—and began rehearsals with the ability to accompany myself. Since then, I have never lived too far from a piano."

What you believe about your own potential for success counts far more than what any other person may believe. Believe what God believes about you— you were created for success.

253

# TRIUMPH IS JUST "UMPH" ADDED TO TRY.

*Whatsoever thy hand findeth to do,*
*do it with thy might.*
*Ecclesiastes 9:10*

Many years ago in England, a small boy grew up speaking with a lisp. He was never a scholar in school. When war broke out involving his nation, he was rejected from service, told that "we need *men.*" He once rose to address the House of Commons, and all present walked out of the room. In fact, he often spoke to empty chairs and echoes. But one day, he became Prime Minister of Great Britain, and with stirring speeches and bold decisions, he led his nation to victory. His name was Sir Winston Churchill.

Many years ago in Illinois, a man with only a few years of formal education failed in business in '31, was defeated in a run for the state legislature in '32, again failed in business in '33, was elected to the legislature in '34, but defeated for speaker in '38. He was defeated for elector in '40, defeated for Congress in '43, elected to Congress in '46, but defeated in '48. He was defeated for Senate in '55, defeated for the vice-presidential nomination in '56, and defeated for the Senate in '58. But in 1860, he was elected president. His name was Abraham Lincoln.

No one is defeated until he gives up trying.

# A GOAL PROPERLY SET IS HALFWAY REACHED.

*And the LORD answered me, and said,*
*Write the vision, and make it plain upon*
*tables, that he may run that readeth it.*
*Habakkuk 2:2*

A young man in need of work once saw this advertisement in a Boston newspaper: "Wanted: young man as an understudy to a financial statistician, P.O. Box 1720." The young man decided this was just the kind of job he wanted, so he replied to the ad but received no answer. He wrote again, and even a third time with no reply. Next, he went to the Boston post office and asked the name of the holder of Box 1720, but the clerk refused to give it, as did the postmaster.

Early one morning, an idea came to the young man. He rose early, took the first train to Boston, went to the post office, and stood watch near Box 1720. After awhile, a man appeared, opened the box and took out the mail. The young man followed him as he returned to the office of a stock brokerage firm. The young man entered and asked for the manager.

In the interview, the manager asked, "How did you find out that I was the advertiser?" The young man told about his detective work, to which the manager replied, "Young man, you are just the kind of persistent fellow I want. You are employed!"

If a goal is worthy, there's no good reason to stop pursuing it! Find something you truly want to do, then go for it with all your heart, mind, and strength.

257

# I THINK THE ONE LESSON I HAVE LEARNED IS THAT THERE IS NO SUBSTITUTE FOR PAYING ATTENTION.

*We ought to give the more earnest heed
to the things which we have heard,
lest at any time we should let them slip.*
*Hebrews 2:1*

Henry P. Davison was a prominent American financier and one-time head of the American Red Cross. He worked his way up from being a poor boy to become president of a large New York City bank.

While he was a cashier of that bank, a would-be robber came to his window, pointed a revolver at him, and passed a check across his window counter. The check was for one million dollars, payable to the Almighty. Davison remained calm, even though he realized the gravity of the situation. In a loud voice, he repeated the words on the check back to the person standing in front of him, emphasizing the "million dollars." Then he graciously asked the would-be robber how he would like to have *the million dollars* for the Almighty. He then proceeded to count out small bills. In the meantime, the suspicion of a guard had been aroused by the strange request he had overheard. He disarmed the robber and prevented the theft.

In later years, Davison was often asked to give his wisdom to others seeking success. He often advised that courtesy, readiness, willingness, and alertness do more for a person than just being smart.

It has been said that one of the skills of a good communicator is the ability to listen. Paying attention to the words and actions of those around you may be the best schooling you'll ever receive.

# A GOOD LISTENER IS NOT ONLY POPULAR EVERYWHERE, BUT AFTER A WHILE HE KNOWS SOMETHING.

*The ear that heareth the reproof*
*of life abideth among the wise.*
*Proverbs 15:31*

An American Indian was once visiting New York City, and as he walked the busy Manhattan streets with a friend from the city, he suddenly stopped, tilted his head to one side, and said, "I hear a cricket."

"You're crazy," his friend said. The Cherokee answered, "No, I hear a cricket. I do! I'm sure of it."

The friend replied, "It's the noon hour. People are jammed on the sidewalks, cars are honking, taxis are whizzing by, the city is full of noise. And you think you can hear a cricket?"

"I'm sure I do," said the visitor. He listened even more closely and then walked to the corner, spotted a shrub in a large cement planter, dug into the leaves underneath it, and pulled out a cricket. His friend was astounded. The man said, "The fact is, my friend, that my ears are different than yours. It all depends on what your ears have been tuned to hear. Let me show you." At that, he reached into his pocket, pulled out a handful of loose change, and dropped the coins on the pavement. Every head within a half block turned. "See what I mean?" he said, picking up the coins. "It all depends on what you are listening for."

Listen today to those things that will make you wise. Don't neglect those things that will prepare you for eternity.

# INDECISION IS OFTEN WORSE THAN THE WRONG ACTION.

*A double minded man is unstable*
*in all his ways.*
*James 1:8*

# God's Little Devotional Book

Former President Ronald Reagan enjoyed telling the following story about himself. He claimed it was how he learned, early in life, to make firm and resolute decisions.

According to the story, a kindly aunt once took him to a cobbler to have a pair of shoes custom-made for him. The shoemaker asked, "Do you want a square toe or a round one?" The young Reagan hemmed and hawed, so the cobbler said, "Come back in a day or two and tell me what you want."

A few days later the cobbler saw Reagan on the street and asked what he had decided about the shoes. "I haven't made up my mind," Reagan answered.

"Very well," the cobbler said, and then he announced to his customer, "Your shoes will be ready tomorrow." When Reagan got the shoes, one had a round toe and the other a square toe!

Reagan concluded, "Looking at those shoes every day taught me a lesson. If you don't make your own decisions, somebody else will make them for you."

Remember always that no decision, is a decision!"

263

# SUCCESS IS NEVER FINAL; FAILURE IS NEVER FATAL; IT IS COURAGE THAT COUNTS.

*Be of good courage, and he shall strengthen*
*your heart, all ye that hope in the* LORD.
*Psalm 31:24*

In *The Seven Habits of Highly Effective People,* Stephen R. Covey writes: "One of the most inspiring times Sandra and I have ever had took place over a four-year period with a dear friend of ours named Carol, who had a wasting cancer disease. She had been one of Sandra's bridesmaids, and they had been best friends for over twenty-five years.

"When Carol was in the very last stages of the disease, Sandra spent time at her bedside helping her write her personal history. She returned from those protracted and difficult sessions almost transfixed by admiration for her friend's courage and her desire to write special messages to be given to her children at different stages in their lives.

"Carol would take as little pain-killing medication as possible, so that she had full access to her mental and emotional faculties. Then she would whisper into a tape recorder or to Sandra directly as she took notes. Carol was so proactive, so brave, and so concerned about others that she became an enormous source of inspiration to many people around her."

In today's world, perhaps one trait is needed desperately. Seek to develop it. It's called *courage*.

# I COUNT HIM BRAVER WHO OVERCOMES HIS DESIRES THAN HIM WHO CONQUERS HIS ENEMIES; FOR THE HARDEST VICTORY IS THE VICTORY OVER SELF.

*I beat my body and make it my slave.*
*1 Corinthians 9:27 NIV*

266

A quiet forest dweller who lived high above an Austrian village in the Alps was hired by a town council to keep the pristine mountain springs—the source of the town's water supply—clear of debris. With faithful regularity, the old man patrolled the hills; clearing away silt and removing leaves and branches from the springs. Over time, the village became prosperous. Mill wheels turned, farms were irrigated, and tourists came. Years passed. Then at a council meeting about the city budget, a member noticed the salary figure for the old man. He asked, "Who is he and why do we keep him on the payroll? Has anybody seen him? For all we know, he might be dead." The council voted to dispense with his services.

For several weeks nothing changed. Then the trees began to shed their leaves. One afternoon, a town citizen noticed a brown tint to the water. Within another week, a slick covered sections of the canals, and a foul odor was detected. Sickness broke out.

The town council called a special meeting, and reversing their error in judgment, rehired the old man. Renewed life soon returned to the village as the sparkling waters returned.

Not everyone's job will make the six o'clock news everyday, but no matter where God places you, do your work unto Him, and He will reward you for your faithfulness.

267

# VISION IS THE WORLD'S MOST DESPERATE NEED. THERE ARE NO HOPELESS SITUATIONS, ONLY PEOPLE WHO THINK HOPELESSLY.

*Where there is no vision, the people perish.*
*Proverbs 29:18*

268

One of the great disasters of history took place in 1271. In that year, Niccolo and Matteo Polo, the father and uncle of Marco Polo, visited Kubla Khan, who was considered the world ruler, with authority over all China, all India, and all of the East.

The Kubla Khan was attracted to the story of Christianity as Niccolo and Matteo told it to him. He said to them, "You shall go to your high priest and tell him on my behalf to send me a hundred men skilled in your religion and I shall be baptized, and when I am baptized all my barons and great men will be baptized and their subjects will receive baptism, too, and so there will be more Christians here than there are in your parts."

Nothing was done, however, in response to what the Kubla Khan had requested. After thirty years, only a handful of missionaries was sent. It was too few, too late.

The West apparently did not have the vision to see the East won to Christ. The mind boggles at the possible ways the world might be different today if thirteenth-century China, India, and the other areas of the orient had been converted to Christianity.

If you lack vision today, ask God for it. He has wonders to reveal to you that you can't yet imagine!

# PEOPLE ARE LONELY BECAUSE THEY BUILD WALLS INSTEAD OF BRIDGES.

*You should be like one big happy family . . .*
*loving one another with tender*
*hearts and humble minds.*
*1 Peter 3:8 TLB*

A fable is told of a young orphan boy who had no family and no one to love him. Feeling sad and lonely, he was walking through a meadow one day when he saw a small butterfly caught in a thorn bush. The more the butterfly struggled to free itself, the deeper the thorns cut into its fragile body. The boy carefully released the butterfly, but instead of flying away, the butterfly transformed into an angel right before his eyes.

The boy rubbed his eyes in disbelief as the angel said, "For your wonderful kindness, I will do whatever you would like." The little boy thought for a moment, and then said, "I want to be happy!" The angel replied, "Very well," and then leaned toward him, whispered in his ear, and vanished.

As the little boy grew up, there was no one in the land as happy as he. When people asked him the secret of his happiness, he would only smile and say, "I listened to an angel when I was a little boy."

On his deathbed, his neighbors rallied around him and asked him to divulge the key to his happiness before he died. The old man finally told them: "The angel told me that everyone, no matter how secure they seemed, no matter how old or young, how rich or poor, had need of me."

You have something to give to everyone you come in contact with today. Build bridges instead of walls!

271

# FORGIVENESS MEANS GIVING UP YOUR RIGHT TO PUNISH ANOTHER.

*When you stand praying, if you hold anything against anyone, forgive him, so that your Father in heaven may forgive you your sins.*
Mark 11:25 NIV

Lloyd John Ogilvie wrote in *Let God Love You,* "The hardest time to be gentle is when we know we are right and someone else is obviously dead wrong. . . . But the greatest temptation for most of us is when someone has failed us and has admitted it, and their destiny or happiness is in our hands. We hold the power to give or refuse a blessing."

"Recently, a dear friend hurt me in both word and action. Each time we met . . . I almost began to enjoy the leverage of being the offended one. His first overtures of restitution were resisted because of the gravity of the judgment I had made. He had taken a key idea I had shared with him in confidence and had developed it as his own before I had a chance to use it. The plagiarism of ideas had been coupled with the use of some of my written material, reproduced under his name. . . . The most difficult thing was to surrender my indignation and work through my hurt. . . . "

"Finally, the Lord got me where he wanted me. . . . His word to me was clear and undeniable, 'Lloyd, why is it so important to you who gets the credit, just so my work gets done?' I gave up my right to be what only God could be as this man's judge and savior. The gentle attitude began to flow."

When we withhold forgiveness, it not only hurts the person we don't want to forgive, it hurts us. Our creativity and joy in life are stifled. When we forgive, we release peace and restoration to the forgiven, and to ourselves.

# THE MOST IMPORTANT SINGLE INGREDIENT IN THE FORMULA OF SUCCESS IS KNOWING HOW TO GET ALONG WITH PEOPLE.

*See that no one pays back evil for evil, but always try to do good to each other and to everyone else.*
*1 Thessalonians 5:15* TLB

# God's Little Devotional Book

Many people today seem to go through their day with their "stingers out," ready to attack others or to defend their position at the slightest provocation. We all do well, however, to consider the full nature of the bees we sometimes seem to emulate.

Bees readily feed each other, sometimes even a bee of a different colony. The worker bees feed the queen bee, who cannot feed herself. They feed the drones during their period of usefulness in the hive. They feed the young. They seem to enjoy this social act of mutual feeding.

Bees cluster together for warmth in cold weather and fan their wings to cool the hive in hot weather, thus working for one another's comfort.

When the time comes for bees to move to new quarters, scouts report back to the group, doing a dance very similar to the one used to report a find of honey. When enough scouts have confirmed the suitability of the new location, the bees appear to make a common decision, take wing, and migrate together—all at the same time—in what we call a swarm.

Only as a last-resort measure of self-defense do bees engage their stingers, and then, never against their fellow bees. We would do well to learn from them!

# EVERYONE THINKS OF CHANGING THE WORLD, BUT NO ONE THINKS OF CHANGING HIMSELF.

*Unless you change and become like little children,*
*you will never enter the kingdom of heaven.*
*Matthew 18:3 NIV*

Andrew Carnegie, considered to be one of the first to emphasize self-esteem and the potential for inner greatness, was famous for his ability to produce millionaires from among his employees. One day a reporter asked him, "How do you account for the fact you have forty-three millionaires working for you?"

Carnegie replied, "They weren't rich when they came. We work with people the same way you mine gold. You have to remove a lot of dirt before you find a small amount of gold."

Andrew Carnegie knew how to bring about change in people. He helped them realize their hidden treasure within, inspired them to develop it, and then watched with encouragement as their lives were transformed.

The philosopher and psychologist William James once said, "Compared to what we ought to be, we are only half awake. We are making use of only a small part of our physical and mental resources. Stating the thing broadly, the human individual thus lives far within his limits. He possesses powers of various sorts which he habitually fails to use."

In other words, most people only develop a fraction of their abilities. Go for a bigger percentage in *your* life. Find the gold within!

277

# COURAGE IS RESISTANCE TO FEAR, MASTERY OF FEAR—NOT ABSENCE OF FEAR.

*Yea, though I walk through the valley of the shadow of death, I will fear no evil: for thou art with me; thy rod and thy staff they comfort me.*
*Psalm 23:4*

# God's Little Devotional Book

Several years ago, a well-known television circus developed an act involving Bengal tigers. The act was performed live before a large audience. One night, the tiger trainer went into the cage with several tigers, and the door was routinely locked behind him. Spotlights flooded the cage, and television cameras moved in close so the audience could see every detail as he skillfully put the tigers through their paces.

In the middle of the performance, the worst happened: the lights went out. For nearly thirty long seconds, the trainer was locked in with the tigers in the darkness. With their superb night vision, the tigers could see him, but he could not see them. Still, he survived. When the lights came back on, he calmly finished his performance.

When the trainer was asked how he felt, he admitted to feeling chilling fear at first, but then, he said, he realized that even though he couldn't see the big cats, *they didn't know he couldn't see them*. He said, "I just kept cracking my whip and talking to them until the lights came on. They never knew I couldn't see them as well as they could see me."

Keep talking back to the tigers of fear that seem to be stalking you. They will obey your voice of faith!

279

# PRAYER IS AN INVISIBLE TOOL WHICH IS WIELDED IN A VISIBLE WORLD.

*The weapons of our warfare are not carnal,*
*but mighty through God to the*
*pulling down of strong holds.*
*2 Corinthians 10:4*

280

Both a major thoroughfare in Tel Aviv and a bridge that spans the Jordan River are named in honor of Viscount Edmund Henry Hynman Allenby, a British solider. As commander of the Egyptian Expeditionary Forces, he outwitted and defeated the Turks in Palestine in 1917 and 1918, conquering Jerusalem without ever firing a single gun.

As a British solider, Allenby was noncommittal about the official British policies concerning the establishment of a Jewish national home, but he did have a deep understanding of the Jews' desire to dwell in Palestine. At a reception in London, he once told how as a little boy, he had knelt to say his evening prayers, repeating with his childhood lisp the words his mother prayed: "And, O Lord, we would not forget Thine ancient people, Israel; hasten the day when Israel shall again be Thy people and shall be restored to Thy favor and to their land."

Allenby concluded, "I never knew then that God would give me the privilege of helping to answer my own childhood prayers."

What you pray today may well be part of tomorrow's work. The world you envision in prayer may well be the world in which you one day will live!

281

# MONEY IS LIKE AN ARM OR LEG: USE IT OR LOSE IT.

*To him who has will more be given . . . and*
*he will have great plenty; but from him who has*
*not, even the little he has will be taken away.*
*Matthew 13:12 TLB*

A strange memorial can be found in the Mount Hope Cemetery of Hiawatha, Kansas. John M. Davis, an orphan, developed a strong dislike for his wife's family and insisted that none of his fortune go to them. He also refused requests that he eventually bequeath his estate for a hospital desperately needed in the area. Instead, after his wife died in 1930, Mr. Davis chose to invest in an elaborate tomb for himself and his wife. The tomb includes a number of statues depicting the couple at various stages of their lives. One statue is of Mr. Davis as a lonely man seated beside an empty chair. It is titled "the vacant chair." Another shows him placing a wreath in front of his wife's tombstone. Many of the statues are made of Kansas granite. No money was left for the memorial's upkeep.

Today, largely because of its weight, this costly memorial is slowly sinking into the ground. It has become weathered and worn from the strong winds in this plains state. The townspeople regard the Davis tomb as an "old man's folly," and many predict that within the next fifty years, the memorial will have become obliterated beyond recognition and will need to be demolished. What could have been a living legacy will eventually become granite dust.

The Bible encourages us many times not to hoard up money to be used for our own selfish desires, but to be kind to the poor. When we do so, God blesses us with more. The more we give, the more we receive, and our legacy will last well into the future instead of sinking into oblivion.

283

# IN TRYING TIMES, DON'T QUIT TRYING.

*The righteous also shall hold on his way,*
*and he that hath clean hands shall*
*be stronger and stronger.*
*Job 17:9*

In 1894, a sixteen-year-old found this note from his rhetoric teacher at Harrow, in England, attached to his report card: "A conspicuous lack of success." The young man kept on trying and went on to become one of the most famous speakers of the twentieth century. His name was Winston Churchill.

In 1902, an aspiring twenty-eight-year-old writer received a rejection letter from the poetry editor of *The Atlantic Monthly*. Returned, with a batch of poems he had sent, was this curt note: "Our magazine has no room for your vigorous verse." He kept on trying, however, and went on to see his work published. The poet's name was Robert Frost.

In 1905, the University of Bern turned down a Ph.D. dissertation as being fanciful and irrelevant. The young physics student, who wrote the dissertation, kept on trying and went on to develop some of his ideas into widely accepted theories. His name was Albert Einstein.

When rejection shakes your resolve and dims your goals, keep on trying. If you do not quit, one day, you will be living out your dreams!

# LET US NOT SAY, "EVERY MAN IS THE ARCHITECT OF HIS OWN FORTUNE;" BUT LET US SAY, "EVERY MAN IS THE ARCHITECT OF HIS OWN CHARACTER."

*Till I die I will not remove mine integrity from me. My righteousness I hold fast, and will not let it go: my heart shall not reproach me so long as I live.*

*Job 27:5-6*

When Chief Justice Charles Evans Hughes moved to Washington, D.C., to take up his duties on the Supreme Court, he transferred his church membership letter to a Baptist church in the area.

It was customary for all new members in this church to come to the front of the sanctuary at the close of the worship service so they might be officially introduced and welcomed. The first person to be called forward that morning was Ah Sing, a Chinese laundryman who had moved to Washington from the West Coast. He took his place at the far side of the church. As the dozen or so others were called forward that day, they came forward and stood on the opposite side of the church, leaving Ah Sing standing alone.

Finally Chief Justice Hughes was called forward, and he immediately made his way to the front and proceeded to stand next to Ah Sing. The minister who welcomed the group into church fellowship said, "I do not want this congregation to miss this remarkable illustration of the fact that at the cross of Jesus Christ, the ground is level."

Your character is shown in many ways, but one of the most obvious is the way you treat people. You will grow in character and reputation if you treat others with kindness.

# IT IS IMPOSSIBLE FOR THAT MAN TO DESPAIR WHO REMEMBERS THAT HIS HELPER IS OMNIPOTENT.

*I will lift up my eyes to the mountains;
From whence shall my help come? My help comes
from the LORD, Who made heaven and earth.
Psalm 121:1-2 NASB*

E. Stanley Jones tells the story of a missionary who became lost in an African jungle. Looking around, he saw nothing but bush and a few clearings. He stumbled about until he finally came across a native hut. He asked one of the natives if he could lead him out of the jungle and back to the mission station. The native agreed to help him.

"Thank you!" exclaimed the missionary. "Which way do I go?" The native replied, "Walk." And so they did, hacking their way through the unmarked jungle for more than an hour.

In pausing to rest, the missionary looked around and had the same overwhelming sense that he was lost. Again, all he could see was bush and a few clearings. "Are you quite sure this is the way?" he asked. "I don't see any path."

The native looked at him and replied, "Bwana, in this place there is no path. I am the path."

When we have no clues about which direction we're going, we must remember that God who guides us is omniscient—all wise. When we run out of time, we must remember that God is omnipresent—all time is in His hand. When we are weak, we must remember that God is omnipotent—all-powerful. He is everything we need.

# A MAN WHO DOES NOT READ GOOD BOOKS HAS NO ADVANTAGE OVER THE MAN WHO *CAN'T* READ THEM.

*Apply thine heart unto instruction, and
thine ears to the words of knowledge.*
*Proverbs 23:12*

After experiencing numerous failures in business and politics, Abraham Lincoln still maintained his daily habit of reading. A critic scoffed, "What good is all that education? It has never earned you a decent living."

Lincoln replied, "Education is not given for the purpose of earning a living; it's learning what to do with a living after you earn it that counts."

One of America's greatest reading advocates is Jim Trelease. He has devoted nearly two decades to promoting what he considers the most important social factor in our lives today. "The more you read," he says, "the smarter you grow. The smarter you grow, the longer you stay in school. The longer you stay in school, the more money you earn. The more you earn, the better your children will do in school. So if you hook a child with reading, you influence not only his future but also that of the next generation."

Reading researchers agree. They have long seen a correlation between the time a person spends reading and the number of innovative ideas and creative solutions a person has. Reading affects a person's ability to reason, and his ability to communicate, by providing an extended and accurate vocabulary.

Spend some time reading today. It will be time well spent, investing in your personal growth, which affects your future success. As the poster often seen hanging in libraries and classrooms says, "Succeed . . . Read!"

291

# THOSE THAT HAVE DONE NOTHING IN LIFE ARE NOT QUALIFIED TO JUDGE THOSE THAT HAVE DONE LITTLE.

*Judge not, and ye shall not be judged:*
*condemn not, and ye shall not be condemned.*
*Luke 6:37*

In the 1700s, an English cobbler kept a map of the world on his workshop wall so that he might be reminded to pray for the nations of the world. As the result of such prayer, he became especially burdened for a specific missionary outreach. He shared this burden at a meeting of ministers, but was told by a senior minister, "Young man, sit down. When God wants to convert the heathen, He will do it without your help or mine."

The cobbler, William Carey, did not let this man's remarks put out the flame of his concern. When he couldn't find others to support the missionary cause that had burdened his soul, he became a missionary himself. His pioneering efforts in India are legendary; his mighty exploits for God are recorded by many church historians.

Be careful how you respond to the enthusiasm of others. Don't dampen someone's zeal for God. Be cautious in how you respond to the new ideas of another, that you don't squelch their God-given creativity.

Be generous and kind in evaluating the work of others, so that you might encourage those things which are worthy. Be slow to judge and quick to praise. Then pray for the same in your own life!

PEOPLE, PLACES, AND THINGS WERE NEVER MEANT TO GIVE US LIFE. GOD ALONE IS THE AUTHOR OF A FULFILLING LIFE.

*I am come that they might have life, and that they might have it more abundantly.*
John 10:10

294

A young man once came to Jesus asking Him what he needed to do to have eternal life. Jesus replied that he should keep the commandments. The young man then claimed that he had always kept them. Jesus advised, *If you would be perfect, sell everything you have, give the money to the poor, and come and follow me (Matthew 19:21).*

The Scriptures tell us that the young man *went away sorrowful: for he had great possessions (vs. 22).* The young man not only had great possessions, but apparently those possessions had him! He couldn't bear to part with earthly, temporary goods in order to obtain heavenly, eternal goods. Jesus also taught, of course, that heaven's "wealth" can be ours now. This young man didn't have to wait until he died to attain the benefits of eternal life. If he had been willing to give up his hold on his "stuff," he could have enjoyed great joy, peace, and fulfillment in life—things he was apparently lacking or he wouldn't have asked Jesus the question.

Take a look at your possessions today. Are there books, tapes, or clothes you can give away to someone in need of learning, inspiration, or clothing? Discover how rewarding giving can be!

# ONE MAN WITH COURAGE MAKES A MAJORITY.

*Be strong and of a good courage . . . for the LORD thy God . . . will not fail thee, nor forsake thee.*
*Deuteronomy 31:6*

296

A teenager named Buck was walking to his father's apartment from a subway stop one day, when he suddenly realized that two men were flanking him.

"Give me your wallet," one of the men insisted. "I have a gun. Give me your wallet, or I'll shoot."

"No," Buck said.

"Hey, man, you don't understand. We're robbing you. Give me your wallet."

"No."

"Give me your wallet, or I'll knife you."

"No."

"Give me your wallet, or we'll beat you up."

By now the robber was pleading more than he was demanding.

"No," Buck said once again. He kept walking, and a few steps later, he realized that the two men had disappeared. As he related this story to a friend, the friend asked, "Weren't you scared?"

Buck replied, "Of course I was scared!"

"Then why didn't you give them your wallet?"

"Because," Buck answered matter-of-factly, "My learner's permit is in it."

While it may be wise to give in to the demands of a thief, the first and best answer to fear is always, "No!"

# YOU WILL NEVER MAKE A MORE IMPORTANT DECISION THAN THE PERSON YOU MARRY.

*Therefore shall a man leave his father and his mother, and shall cleave unto his wife: and they shall be one flesh.*

*Genesis 2:24*

When Ruth Bell was a teenager, she was sent from her childhood home in China to school in Korea. At the time, she fully intended to follow in her parents' footsteps and become a missionary. She envisioned herself a confirmed "old maid," ministering to the people of Tibet. While at school, however, Ruth did give some serious thought to the kind of husband that she *might* consider. As she tells in her book *A Time for Remembering,* she listed these particulars:

"If I marry: He must be so tall that when he is on his knees, as one has said, he reaches all the way to heaven. His shoulders must be broad enough to bear the burden of a family. His lips must be strong enough to smile, firm enough to say no, and tender enough to kiss. Love must be so deep that it takes its stand in Christ and so wide that it takes the whole lost world in. He must be active enough to save souls. He must be big enough to be gentle and great enough to be thoughtful. His arms must be strong enough to carry a little child."

Ruth Bell never did become a full-time missionary in Tibet. However, she did find a man worth marrying—Billy Graham. As his wife, Ruth Bell Graham became a missionary to the whole world!

Your spouse will be the most important person in your life. It's crucial to marry the right person. Think about the qualities that you would like to have in a mate. If you haven't already, begin to pray for the person you will eventually marry. Even if you haven't met him or her yet, God knows who they are.

CLASS OF 2000

299

# THE BIBLE HAS A WORD TO DESCRIBE "SAFE" SEX: IT'S CALLED MARRIAGE.

*Marriage should be honored by all, and the
marriage bed kept pure, for God will judge
the adulterer and all the sexually immoral.*

*Hebrews 13:4 NIV*

The 1960s were known for many rebellions, among them the sexual revolution. "Free love" spilled from the hippie movement into the mainstream American culture. Premarital sexual relations sanctioned by the "new morality" became openly flaunted.

One of the unexpected results of this trend, however, received little publicity. As reported by Dr. Francis Braceland, past president of the American Psychiatric Association and editor of the *American Journal of Psychiatry,* an increasing number of young people were admitted to mental hospitals during that time. In discussing this finding at a National Methodist Convocation of Medicine and Theology, Braceland concluded, "A more lenient attitude on campus about premarital sexual experience has imposed stresses on some college women severe enough to cause emotional breakdown."

Looking back over the years since the "new morality" was sanctioned by a high percentage of the American culture, one finds a rising number of rapes, abortions, divorces, premarital pregnancies, single-family homes, and cases of sexually transmitted diseases, including herpes and HIV.

The evidence is compelling: the old morality produced safer, healthier, and happier people!

# NOTHING IS EVER LOST BY COURTESY. . . . IT PLEASES HIM WHO GIVES AND HIM WHO RECEIVES, AND THUS, LIKE MERCY, IT IS TWICE BLESSED.

*So then, while we have opportunity,*
*let us do good to all men.*
*Galatians 6:10 NASB*

We often refer to courtesy as "common courtesy," but it is far from common these days. In fact, it is pretty rare. How many people do you know who follow the basic common courtesies given in this section?

A father once remarked about his three children: "My children may not be the brightest children in their class. They may not be the most talented or the most skilled. They may not achieve great fame, or earn millions of dollars. But by my insisting that they have good manners, I know they will be welcome in all places and by all people." How true!

Good manners—exhibiting common courtesies—are like a calling card. They open doors that are otherwise shut to those who are rude, crude, or unmannerly. They bring welcome invitations, and quite often, return engagements. They cover a multitude of weaknesses and flaws. They make other people feel good about themselves, and they in turn, extend kindness and generosity they might not otherwise exhibit. Good manners are a prerequisite for good friendships, good business associations, and good marriages. It is a key to success!

# THE MEASURE OF SUCCESS IS NOT WHETHER YOU HAVE A TOUGH PROBLEM TO DEAL WITH, BUT WHETHER IT'S THE SAME PROBLEM YOU HAD LAST YEAR.

*But the God of all grace, who hath called us unto his eternal glory by Christ Jesus, after that ye have suffered a while, make you perfect, stablish, strengthen, settle you.*

*1 Peter 5:10*

For years, farmers in southern Alabama had one mainstay crop: cotton. They plowed as much ground as they could each year to plant their big cash crop, and year after year, they lived by their cotton production. Then one year, the dreaded boll weevil devastated the entire area's crops. Optimistic that the tragedy was an isolated event, the farmers mortgaged their homes and planted cotton again the next year, hoping for a big harvest to help them recoup their losses. But once again, the insect destroyed the crop, and as a result, most of the farmers were wiped out.

The few farmers who were able to survive two years of boll weevil infestation decided to do something they had never done before the third year—plant peanuts. The peanuts proved to be resistant to insects, and the market was strong. Most of those who planted peanuts were able to reap enough profit that third year to pay off all their debts. They chose to plant peanuts from that point on, and they greatly prospered.

In the following years, the farmers actually erected a monument to their old enemy, the boll weevil. They concluded that if it hadn't been for the boll weevil, they never would have discovered peanuts.[6]

If a problem forces you to take a detour, don't be discouraged. You may find it is a better road!

# CHILDREN WHO BRING HONOR TO THEIR PARENTS REAP BLESSINGS FROM THEIR GOD.

*Honor your father and your mother,*
*so that you may live long in the land*
*the LORD your God is giving you.*
*Exodus 20:12 NIV*

A mother watched with raised eyebrows as her two sons took a hammer and a few nails from the kitchen utility drawer and scurried to one of the boys' rooms, giggling and talking in low voices. When she didn't hear any hammering, she continued with her chores. Then from the kitchen window, she saw one of the boys take a stepladder from the garage. He disappeared from sight before she could call to him. A few minutes later her other son came into the kitchen to ask if she had any rope. "No," Mom said. "What's going on?" Her son said, "Nothin'." Mom pressed, "Are you sure?" But her son was out of sight.

Highly suspicious, Mom went to her son's room. She found the door closed and locked. She knocked. "What are you boys doing in there?" she asked. One son replied, "Nothin'." Suspecting great mischief, she demanded entrance. "I want you to open this door right now!" she said. A few seconds later, the door popped open, and her son shouted, "Surprise!" as he handed her a rather crudely wrapped present. "Happy birthday, Mom!" the other boy added. Truly surprised, the mother stammered, "But what about the hammer, nails, ladder, and rope?" The boys grinned, "Those were just decoys, Mom."

# THOSE WHO DESIRE TO LEAD MUST FIRST LEARN TO RESPECT AUTHORITY AND OBEY.

*Show respect for everyone. Love Christians everywhere. Fear God and honor the government.*
*1 Peter 2:17* TLB

While driving down a country road, a man came to a very narrow bridge. In front of the bridge, there was a sign that read, "Yield." Seeing no oncoming cars, the man continued across the bridge and to his destination. On his way back this same route, he came to the same one-lane bridge, now from the opposite direction. To his surprise, he saw another "Yield" sign posted there.

Curious, he thought, *I'm sure there was one positioned on the other side.* Sure enough, when he reached the other side of the bridge and looked back, he saw the sign. Yield signs had been placed at both ends of the bridge, obviously with the intent that drivers from both directions were requested to give each other the right-of-way. It was a reasonable and doubly sure way to prevent a head-on collision.

If you find yourself in a combative situation with someone who has more authority than you—or equal authority—it is always wise to yield to them. If they indeed have more authority, a lack of submission will put you in a position to be punished or reprimanded. If you are of equal authority, an exercise of your power will only build resentment in a person better kept as an ally. As the Bible says, we are to *prefer one another (Romans 12:10).*

# SUCCESS CONSISTS OF GETTING UP MORE TIME THAN YOU FALL.

*Though a righteous man falls*
*seven times, he rises again.*
*Proverbs 24:16 NIV*

Ray Charles has been able to do what few musicians can—create music that appeals to young and old, black and white, rich and poor. He successfully crosses major boundaries.

Charles lost both parents and a brother before he was grown. He grew up in a school for the blind, where he learned to play piano and sing. By his late teens, he was a hit in central and north Florida. His friends believed in his talent, and Charles believed in them. In 1946, when Lucky Millinder's band arrived in Orlando, Charles managed to get an audition. It was his first chance at the big time.

Charles sang and played with all his might. Millinder listened quietly. At the end of the audition, as Charles expected to hear praise, all he heard was silence and then finally these devastating words, "Ain't good enough, kid." Charles thought he had heard incorrectly and asked Millinder to repeat what he had said. "You heard me. You don't got what it takes." Charles later said of the incident, "I went back to my room and cried for days."

In retrospect, Charles considers that blow to be the "best thing that ever happened to me. After I got over feeling sorry for myself, I went back and started practicing, so nobody would ever say that about me again."[7]

Everybody takes a hit sometime. The successful bounce back.

311

# IT'S NOT ENOUGH TO GET ALL THE BREAKS. YOU'VE GOT TO KNOW HOW TO USE THEM.

*He who gathers crops in summer is a wise son, but he who sleeps during harvest is a disgraceful son.*
Proverbs 10:5 NIV

The header reads "God's Little Devotional Book"

Header is a banner graphic with title text.

# God's Little Devotional Book

Shortly after moving into a new home a number of years ago, a family was besieged by salesmen offering everything from laundry service to life insurance. One busy day a dairyman came to their door. "No," the woman of the house said firmly, "my husband and I don't drink milk."

"I'd be glad to deliver a quart every morning for cooking," the salesman said. "That's more than I need," she replied, starting to close the door. "Well, ma'am, how about some cream? Berries comin' in now, and . . . " She said curtly, "No, we never use cream."

The dairyman slowly retreated, and the woman congratulated herself on her sales resistance. The fact was, she had already ordered from another dairy and had simply taken the easy way out. The next morning, however, the same dairyman appeared at her door, a bowl of dewy ripe strawberries held carefully in one hand a half-pint bottle of cream in the other. "Lady," he said, as he poured the cream over the berries and handed them to her, "I got to thinkin'—you sure have missed a lot!" Needless to say, she switched dairies.[8]

You haven't exhausted all of your opportunities until you've tapped all your creativity—and creativity is an inexhaustible resource!

313

# GOD HAS GIVEN MAN ONE TONGUE BUT TWO EARS THAT WE MAY HEAR TWICE AS MUCH AS WE SPEAK.

*Do not keep talking so proudly or
let your mouth speak such arrogance.*
*1 Samuel 2:3 NIV*

Mr. Brown was in his final year of seminary, preparing to become a pastor. The policy of his school called for him to be available at a moment's notice to fill in for local churches who might need a preacher. Mr. Brown eagerly awaited such an opportunity, and at long last, his moment arrived. The pastor of a country church was called away on an emergency, and Mr. Brown was asked to fill the pulpit.

Having waited so long for the opportunity, and having so much to say, Mr. Brown soon became completely immersed in his own words. The more he preached, the more he became inspired to preach. When he glanced at his watch, he was shocked to see that he had preached for a full hour. He was truly embarrassed since he had been allotted only thirty minutes to preach. Knowing that he had preached well into the lunch hour, he made a heartfelt apology to the congregation and sat down.

A young woman hurried to him after the service ended. Obviously more impressed with his personality and appearance—and perhaps his availability—than she was with his message, she gushed, "Oh, Brother Brown, you needn't have apologized. You really didn't talk long—it just seemed long."

The old rule of thumb is, "Always leave them wanting more."

315

# YOU CANNOT STEAL SECOND BASE WHILE KEEPING ONE FOOT ON FIRST BASE.

*A double minded man is unstable in all his ways.*

*James 1:8*

316

Most baseball fans know that from 1960 to 1966, the record for the most stolen bases was held by Maury Wills of the Los Angeles Dodgers. In 1962, Wills seemed to set fire to the path between first and second, stealing 104 bases in one season.

Maury Wills set another record during those same years—a rather dubious one. In 1965, a year in which he held the top honors for the most stolen bases, he also held the record for being thrown out the most times while attempting to steal a base! He was caught trying to steal thirty-one times that year.

We don't really remember the bases Wills *didn't* steal, only the ones he did. But the fact is, had Maury Wills allowed himself to become discouraged at being thrown out, he never would have set the records he did. He was a man determined to "go for it," to do his best, to take the risk of trying, to push the envelope a little in the lead he took off first base, to get a jump on the pitch and fly to second base in a race against the catcher. Once Wills set out to steal a base, there was *no turning back*.

Whatever it is you desire to do today, do it with your whole heart and all your determination—no looking back.

# Endnotes

1. *Design for Living,* Clinton T. Howell (NY: Grosset & Dunlap, 1970), p. 39.

2. *Reader's Digest,* February, 1994, p. 119.

3. *Illustrations Unlimited,* James S. Hewett, ed. (Wheaton, IL: Tyndale, 1988), p. 185.

4. *One Door Closes, Another Door Opens,* Arthur Pine (NY: Dell Trade Paperback, 1993), pp. 60, 61.

5. *Illustrations Unlimited,* James S. Hewett, ed. (Wheaton, IL: Tyndale, 1988), p. 469, 470.

6. *Illustrations for Preaching and Teaching,* Craig Brian Larson (Grand Rapids, MI: Baker Books, 1993), p. 7.

7. *The Achievement Factors,* B. Eugene Griessman (NY: Dodd, Mead & Co., 1987), pp. 54, 55.

8. *Illustrations Unlimited,* James S. Hewett, ed. (Wheaton, IL: Tyndale, 1988), p. 469.

# Acknowledgments

We acknowledge and thank the following people for the quotes used in this book: Albert Einstein (8), Diane Ravich (10), Edward Young (12), Ronald Brown (14), Jim Patrick (16), Harry Emerson Fosdick (18, 204), Calvin Coolidge (20, 210), Sprat (26), Les Brown (28), John D. Rockefeller Jr. (30), Dr. Eugene Swearingen (32, 36, 298), Thomas Jefferson (34), Robert C. Edward (38), C.W. Wendte (40), Arthur Ashe (42), Kin Hubbard (48), Henry Ward Beecher (50, 246), John A. Shedd (54, 74), Ralph Waldo Emerson (58, 160), Dwight L. Moody (60), Ed Cole (64, 280), H.E. Jansen (66), Roy Disney (76), Descartes (78), Helen Keller (80), Seneca (82), Aristotle (84, 162, 266), A.L. Williams (88), William A. Ward (90), Charles H. Spurgeon (92, 124), Moliere (96), Bob Bales (98), Solon (100), Charles C. Noble (102), Samuel Johnson (104, 292), Eleanor Roosevelt (106), John Sculley (108), George Bernard Shaw (110), Oprah Winfrey (112), Thomas Jefferson (116), Benjamin Franklin (120, 224), Woodrow Wilson (122), William Lyon Phelps (126), Washington Irving (128), Terence (132), Henry Wadsworth Longfellow (144), Josh Billings (146), Jean Paul Richter (150), Marvin Feldman (152), Samuel Butler (154), H.P. Liddon (156), George Elliot (158), John R. Rice (164), William H. Danforth (166, 186), Thomas A. Edison (168), Orlando A. Battista (170, 202), George Edward Woodberry (172), Ronald E. Osborn (174), Bill Cosby (176), Winston Churchill (178, 264), Thomas Carlyle (182), Bacon (184), Lillian Dickson (188), Denis Diderot (190), Earl Nightingale (192, 250), Horace (194), Louis D. Brandeis (196), Hannah More (198), Syrus (200), Victor Hugo (206), David Dunn (208), Mark Twain (212, 278), Roy L. Smith (214), Chinese Proverb (216), Oliver Wendell Holmes (218), Johann Wolfgang von Goethe (220), George Washington (222), Parks Robinson (228), George Sala (230), Say (232), Cervantes (234), Ben Patterson (240), James Whitcomb Riley (242), Zig Ziglar (244, 256), Builder (248), Abraham Lincoln (252), Diane Sawyer (258), Wilson Mizner (260), George P. Burnham (262), Winifred Newman (268), Joseph Newton (270), Dennis Rainey (272), Theodore Roosevelt (274), Leo Tolstoy (276), Henry Ford (282), George Dana Boardman (286), Jeremy Taylor (288), Margaret Fuller (290), Gary Smalley & John Trent (294, 300), Erastus Wiman (302), Oliver Goldsmith (310), Huey P. Long (312), John A. Shedd (314).

Additional copies of this book and other
titles in the *God's Little Devotional Book* series
are available from your local bookstore.

*God's Little Devotional Book*
*God's Little Devotional Book for Students*
*God's Little Devotional Book for Graduates*
*God's Little Devotional Book for Dads*
*God's Little Devotional Book for Moms*
*God's Little Devotional Book for Men*
*God's Little Devotional Book for Couples*

If you have enjoyed this book, or if it has impacted
your life, we would like to hear from you.

Please contact us at:
Honor Books
Department E
P. O. Box 55388
Tulsa, Oklahoma 74155

Honor Books
Tulsa, Oklahoma